Shortcuts to Beginning Reading

A How-To Manual

Marie L. Myers

The Scarecrow Press, Inc.
Lanham, Md., & London
1996

SCARECROW PRESS, INC.

Published in the United States of America
by Scarecrow Press, Inc.
4720 Boston Way
Lanham, Maryland 20706

4 Pleydell Gardens, Folkestone
Kent CT20 2DN, England

British Cataloguing-in-Publication Information Available

Library of Congress Cataloging-in-Publication Data

Myers, Marie L., 1944–
    Shortcuts to beginning reading : a how-to manual / by Marie L.
Myers.
       p. cm.
    Includes bibliographical references and index.
    ISBN 0-8108-3213-5 (pbk : alk. paper)
    1. Reading (Elementary) 2. Children—Books and reading.
  I. Title.
LB1573.M94   1996
372.41—dc20   96–9173
                                            CIP

ISBN 0–8108–3213–5 (pbk : alk. paper)

To my Parents,
Paul and Ruth,
who taught me to love reading

Contents

Preface

Pete was a rebellious sixth-grade orphan being cared for by an old friend of mine in another state. He was a slow, jerky reader who "couldn't concentrate at all." His teacher discovered that his interests were fast vehicles and the physical principles behind that speed. Pete complained that whenever he did find books about his hobby, he could not read them. His teacher hunted and found a book about rocket-propelled vehicles in story format with a vocabulary only slightly above Pete's independent reading level (see glossary).

Pete's mom watched the methods the teacher used to teach Peter to read and then spent three hours per week using the same methods with similar books in Pete's interest category. First the teacher read a paragraph to Pete while he read silently. Then she read the paragraph aloud again, after which he, too, read it aloud. When this was mastered, she read a page, after which he read the same page, first silently and then aloud. They next alternated reading pages. Pete's mom practiced the same methods with him at home, giving Pete access to many library books that had previously frustrated him. It was the only way of reaching Pete, who hated "Dick-and-Jane" stories.

Pete's was a success story, thanks to techniques such as those discussed in this handbook—a how-to manual of strategies to teach reading much like the ones used with Pete. The manual cuts through theory and outlines very simply (but *not* simplistically!), in "shortcut" form, what to do to learn how to read. The emphasis is on *fluency,* or reading that flows naturally and automatically, because if a reader's attention is expended primarily on trying to figure out a word, he or she cannot understand the meaning of the text (Wilson 1988). If you want to know how to get started, this book is for you.

While the procedures are presented for beginning readers, most are helpful for any age reader, from kindergarten to adult. Teachers can refer parents to this manual as a supplement to the school reading program. Parents who wish to teach their children at home may use these methods to get their children started reading or to help strengthen good reading habits in older children. Adults who wish to improve their reading fluency or who teach adult learners will be more successful if they incorporate many of the suggestions included. Even librarians may find many of the ideas helpful.

This manual suggests methods that have worked consistently for me in reading classes in many settings, including the home school. The methods are a healthy sampling of those recommended in today's research on literacy-based, whole language, phonics, and basal reading instruction. The principles on which the methods are based cut across program lines; I do not present any one program in reading, but rather timeless principles generic to any balanced reading program. These principles are not eclectic—they are merely good reading practice, based on current research (see chapter 1).

In order to simplify the "goodies" in the field of reading, I have synthesized a repertoire of methods and ways to implement them that should work for the average reading student, and I have written them so that lay people, as well as teachers, can use them.

What This Manual Is About

This manual emphasizes good fluency-building skills. The definition of fluency I like to use is "reading at a rate at which the student comprehends easily." Although it is impossible to separate fluency from comprehension, this book concentrates primarily on methods that build fluency, since fluency seems to be critical to comprehension. Criteria for methods included depended mainly on whether the strategy built fluency, but readers are encouraged to read the many good books that emphasize comprehension-building strategies, such as pre-and post-reading discussion questions.

The target audience for this manual is tutors, parents, and teachers of any readers who do not suffer from neurological or biological impairments.

Because the book focuses on "getting them reading," other components of a language arts plan herein presented are mentioned only as they relate to the *automaticity* (fluent, free-flowing, instant reading at an appropriate pace) and speed of the reading process. However, the reading methods in chapter 3 can easily be integrated with one's choice of evaluation procedures, writing skills, and other areas of language arts instruction.

Undergirding Philosophy

A major presupposition of this book is that the students benefitting from it are ready to read—that is, they know the alphabet and can identify letter-sound relationships, recognize similarity of shapes, and easily distinguish between dissimilar shapes.

Although the rationale and philosophy are more fully explained in chapter 1, the reader should know that the primary emphasis and goal of this book is *fluency.* If a reader is fluent—that is, he or she recognizes words automatically without having to stop to decode—many of the other comprehension-building and language arts strategies can more easily follow.   Thus,   I   do   not emphasize phonics, although phonics is certainly a help to the   beginning   reader.   A   minimum   of   phonics   is covered—only those the beginning reader is apt to remember and access quickly. These helps are mentioned in chapter 3. I feel that other phonics rules should be taught after fluency is achieved at a very basic level. For a more complete discussion on phonics and philosophy, refer to chapter 1.

I subscribe to the "Get 'em Reading First" philosophy. It is important, especially for a child going to school on the first day who expects to come home reading, to give that child   a   successful   reading   experience   that   very   day. Although I do not enter the sticky debate about whether or not students should learn all letter sounds and/or vowels before they learn sight words, I highly recommend teaching a few meaningful sight words the first day. I also recognize the importance of learning consonants and possibly long and short vowel sounds early on.

Sight reading has been under-appreciated and under-explored as a method for learning to read. Chapter 1 discusses the rationale for requiring beginning readers to build a strong sight vocabulary with a few well-learned phonics rules at first, increasing phonics as fluency is acquired.

How Do I Know at Which Level to Begin?

The literature speaks of independent, instructional, and frustration levels of reading: the independent level is attained when readers understand and recognize 98% of the vocabulary and need little or no help; the instructional level is gained when a reader needs some support or prereading help with new words; and the frustration level is reached when material is very tough or too difficult, such as when a fourth grader tries to read a manual for fixing a car.

To build fluency, readers should begin reading at their independent level. New words should be introduced only as the former "new" words are mastered to the level of automaticity.

How to Build Fluency

Fluency involves a high proportion of reading at the independent level and a small proportion of reading at the instructional level.

The key to building fluency and automaticity in reading is *rereading,* a basic sight method that, in my opinion, should be more fully explored and utilized by beginning readers. If one were to lay this book down and merely reread selections at his or her independent level three or four times, with the aid of a tape recorder or good reader if necessary, fluency would likely be the result.

This manual is also based on the premise that words are remembered more easily and permanently if they are learned *in context* rather than in isolation. In order to be recognized, a word must have meaning. Research shows that students memorize and remember passages better if they learn words in a paragraph or on a page that is a part of a larger story or essay, thus giving meaning to the words being mastered. Finally, beginning readers must read vocabulary they can use and understand. City children may have a much easier time understanding a story about a favorite television hero than one about raising a prize-winning animal for the 4-H Club Fair.

A cardinal rule that summarizes how to build fluency might be: if one *sees*, *understands*, and *knows* the *sound* of a word and repeats the association of sight, hearing, and understanding enough times in close enough sequence, one will recognize that word automatically.

How to Use This Book

The first chapter is an overview. Chapter 1 discusses the rationale and research base for the philosophy behind this book; however, it must be remembered that there is not a research base for everything in this manual. Some of the techniques arise out of personal experience in working with readers over the past thirty years.

Chapter 2 outlines various ways to implement the methods into a customized reading program. Additional ideas and suggestions are offered so that different readers can get a feel for the kinds of procedures they might follow in planning a program that might work for their needs. Such a program might be as simple as rereading a story three times per day or planning the first week of a first-grade reading class. After reading chapter 2, readers and teachers should be able to begin a reading program that will produce a fluent reader.

Chapter 3 consists of various methods a reader or teacher can use. They are listed alphabetically and are described in enough detail to be put into practice immediately. A short paragraph gives a rationale for each method and/or explains under what circumstances the method is best used. This chapter can be used as a reference guide, much like a command summary for use with a computer or word processor.

Chapter 4 offers suggested resources for those who need or wish to gather more materials for their own or others' use in reading. Although not exhaustive, a list of computer software and implementation suggestions that would help add spark and variety to any reading program are included.

One final caveat before you begin: it is my greatest hope that you and your students will *enjoy* reading. If any activities become tedious, put them aside for a while or try a different approach, but be sure your students love reading!

1

What You Need to Know About Learning to Read

Upon meeting a reading teacher, a young mother once said, "Oh, you're a reading teacher? Well, I sure need help. I have a smart five-year-old who's determined to read. She gets so frustrated when I tell her to just read the pictures. So, I finally gave in to her. I read a sentence first; then she reads it, or sometimes we read a book together if it's simple enough. Now, how might I have damaged her?"

The reading teacher replied, "How is it working?"

She responded, "Oh, she reads books by herself now. She reads the same stories over and over, and sometimes she wants me to read new books until she memorizes them, and then she reads them. She loves it, but is she really reading, or is she just memorizing?"

The answer is, she probably used memorizing as a legitimate step in the process of learning to read, and by now she is "really reading." Sometimes parents by instinct do what is best for their beginning readers.

The rationale in this chapter is one of common sense, much like that used by the parent above. I cannot rely on a preponderance of research results to "prove" or back this strategy: as far as I know, no one has done, in a major study, the particular plan I have in mind. Parts and pieces, yes, but not the combination I propose and have tried with excellent results on a small scale.

This chapter is often a foreboding one that many would prefer to skip over. However, we know that "a man convinced against his will is of the same opinion still," and teachers, parents, librarians, and other adults may need to know the "why" for this preferred arrangement for teaching reading, especially the role of phonics.

Here are the mainstays of this strategy and its rationales. If it makes sense to you, try it—I think it will work best. If you do not care for the overall philosophy, you may still find the book useful as a composite of methods that many reading researchers and teachers are using and promoting.

How Do Readers Learn to Read?

Were reading a matter of learning rules and applying them very quickly (fast enough to maintain comprehension and interest while decoding), then it would pay to learn all the phonics rules that future teachers usually do not encounter until their college education courses. Using yourself as an experimental subject, ask, "Beyond the consonant sounds, how many phonics rules can I write down, with their exceptions? Of these, how many do I generally use?"

Reading is basically a process of *simultaneously seeing a word, hearing the word* (in one's head or out loud), *and understanding a word.* Reading is learned by first having a word meaningfully used in spoken language and then introduced visually, aurally, and comprehensively in some pertinent context. This process is repeated over and over within a short enough time frame so that the word is not forgotten between "sightings."

This basic principle of how words are recognized is the foundation of the graduated textbook—the preprimer starts out with just one word, then two, then three, and so on. New words are gradually introduced, so as to be well learned before other words are added.

Reading skill is gained by *repetition,* with new words added very gradually, incrementally, and meaningfully only as the old ones are mastered. For this reason, one grand principle that reinforces many other reading principles is *rereading.* In my classrooms, rereading was the rule, not the exception. Occasionally a selection might be passed with no or only one rereading, but at the beginning, readers need much practice.

The overall strategy of this book is based on *principles* of learning to read, not on beliefs about reading that are historically cyclic and varying in popularity, funding, and consensus. The following statement, a summary of these principles, encapsulates this whole book, for if you really understand it and do what it says, your students will learn to read. Reading is basically a process of simultaneously seeing, hearing, and understanding a word automatically.

Principles of Learning
Relevant to Beginning Reading

Students learn reading and language most rapidly when:

1. They are successful, progress rapidly, and have strong teacher and parental or significant other approval.

2. There is a direct connection between their own life interests and their study tasks at school.

3. They thoroughly enjoy the helpful or "fun" outcome of reading.

4. They know ahead of time (by sight, sounds, and meaning) the new words they will meet in the day's assignment.

5. There is a clear relationship between today's learning and the whole of their lives as they perceive it—past, present, and future. Fragmented, unrelated, irrelevant, isolated bits are frustratingly difficult to retain.

6. They feel "efficient." This negates:

    -tiresome procedures and busywork
    -waiting for teachers and classmates
    -pushing students beyond their limits of
     understanding and speed.

7. There are few environmental distractions (not even from a "helpful" teacher who keeps interrupting their reading).

8. They are not asked to expend so much effort on "rules for reading" or "rules for decoding" that they cannot enjoy the ideas of the content as a whole.

9. Clarity and organization of directives and procedures leaves time for respectful relationships.

10. Broad "theme topics" can serve as organizers for subtopics and their interrelatedness. This facilitates a holistic and systematic relationship of facts and ideas.

11. They sometimes share in the creation of the material they read.

12. It is "safe" to attempt oral responses (because learners are individually asked to read only things they have practiced, and they can join in unison responses wherever they feel able to do so).

13. New learning overlaps with a high proportion of previous learning.

14. They begin independent practice only after having demonstrated around 90% competence (so they do not practice errors).

15. They are asked to drill only with material they understand.

16. They are constantly involved in learning (via direct instruction, monitored practice, peer learning interactions, or meaningful individual quests, creation, and problem-solving).

17. They can pretest out of learning material they already know.

18.   They divide their time between cooperative groups, teams, and individual work (as opposed to the all-or-nothing systems).

19.   Most skills are learned in context of meaningful whole passages, pages, chapters, or books.

20.   They have mastered and utilized past learning, so they expect present learning to also prove satisfying.

21.   They recognize most words without having to interrupt reading to recall and select phonics rules by which to decode.

22.   Newly-learned material is repeated often enough, in a short time frame, so that it is not forgotten between exposures and is quickly memorized.

23.   They spend more time building fluency by seeing correct sentences in meaningful contexts than doing exercises which require them to read incorrect responses in order to select suitable ones.

24.   They recognize sight, sound, and meaning of new words simultaneously, due to a supporting system of prompts, cues, and prerequisite learning.

25.   They utilize mastered material (but are not bored by still practicing it) or else move on.

26.   As beginning readers, they very quickly build up a core of common "sight words" (automatic instant recognition) and high-meaning uncommon words, so

that core words are *instantly* recognized as whole words, not as linked word parts.

27. They are asked to analyze and synthesize only material that is thoroughly understood, even overlearned.

28. They obey clear directives promptly and habitually, so the atmosphere and the relationships are not clouded by nagging, hinting, reminding, frowning, sulking, negotiating, justifying, manipulating, pleading, persuading, threatening, etc. Where intrinsic motivation for students to cooperate is lacking, reasonable positive and negative consequences are supplied.

29. Students usually express some response to what they read—via journal, discussion partner, personal application, group discussion, family discussion, art form, product, activity, teacher conference, or personal reflection.

30. Credit is sometimes (or usually) given for practice, enrichment, helping, and cooperating, to approximately the same extent given for academic final products. (Only unusually fine students are willing to expend much effort and persist in helping behaviors when no external rewards are available.)

31. Learning is multisensory, multimodal.

32. Their reading material is so intensely interesting (even suspenseful, and usually narrative) that they are internally driven to habits of high concentration

and high comprehension. (Ideally, distractions are not as enticing as reading matter.)

33.   Instruction is intensely focused on rapid gain in reading fluency *before* the student is expected to learn content from content-area reading (so no student has to haltingly struggle through uncomprehended content-area reading, and because content-area reading does not build fluency like narrative reading does). Because content-area reading that is limited to very few words can be so boring as to turn the child against reading, it may be best to build high fluency through narratives first.

34.   Rereading material that is not totally clear to the student after the first reading is promoted, routine, and rewarded. The first time the student reads a passage, he or she must gradually, inductively link incomplete pieces in search for an overall meaning. During the second reading, comprehension of the whole gives a frame of reference for instant word recognition, deductive reasoning, and efficient associating of ideas. Subsequent re-reading enables more related ideas to associate in the short-term memory at the same moment, maximizing comprehension.

35.   The student is asked to predict what he or she will read in a passage only when he or she has a strong evidence base on which to make a prediction and justify it. (Teacher-prompted wild guessing reinforces and justifies student acceptance of wild guessing as a valid mode of thinking.) The widely-promoted reading practice of asking students to

predict should not close their minds to new ideas unrelated to the anticipatory set.

Phonics Rationale

Presumably, you have finished reading the first part of this chapter. What percentage of the words did you recognize instantly? ___ %. What percentage of the words did you read by sounding them out? ___ %. Did you read the chapter by phonetic decoding or by instant word recognition? After they read a passage at or near their independent reading level, hundreds of adults of whom I have asked that question have said they instantly recognized about 98% of the words and barely paused over less familiar words.

Had you read the initial section of chapter 1 totally by phonetic decoding, you would have had to have memorized hundreds of phonics rules and their exceptions. You would have had to study each word, decide which rules applied (you have to remember all the rules), apply the rules or detect the exceptions, and then try to remember the previous words in the sentence and paragraph to make sense of or incorporate the meaning of the last word you read. How much would you have enjoyed or comprehended your reading?

For an example of the difficulty in reading by applying memorized phonics rules, let's look at the inconsistency of the words containing just one vowel—"O"—in the chart on the next page.

How many phonics rules, and rules which tell the exceptions to the rules, would it take to read the O words by phonetic decoding?

The Sounds of O

Read down columns (left to right)

stood	bone	shore
took		chore
book	*Oh well...*	more
wood	come	pore
hood		
so far so	dome	pour
good!		
	grown	tour
OK—but then		
hoot	groan	poor
toot	loan	
boot		*No! try*
food	*Let's try*	role
	Ford	stole
blood	bored	hole
whoops!		mole
	board	sole
bud	roared	
oh!		soul
	lord	
money	lowered	*Ouch!*
won		bowl
	warred	know
one		glow
	floor	tow
on	door	
		At last!
gone	wore	mow
	bore	show
stone	store	snow

row (all in a)	though	*How about*
		double
row (ruckus)	thought	trouble
now		
how	taught	stubble
borrow	love	*Maybe these*
sorrow	dove (bird)	*will work...*
		work
sorrel	dove (dive)	word
	drove	
road		port
	move	
rode		*Guess not!*
	people	to
hoed		
	peephole	too
mowed		
sowed	steeple	two
bowed (bent)		
	coy	shoe
bowed (curtsy)		
plowed	coil	do
proud	bound	you
loud	hound	
couch	sound	*Whew!*
	wound (wind)	womb
touch		tomb
	wound (hurt)	
such		bomb
	would	
Let's try		comb
through	wood	*Enough?*

And, if you are looking through the eyes of the beginning reader to ascertain how many phonics rules he or she would need to decode these words by rules, you will have to think also of all the words which are not listed here. The reader has to differentiate each word from every other word, each rule from every other rule.

How can we expect a six-year-old to do this? Many cannot. And many adults cannot. Adults tend to think, "I do not need phonics very often now, because I just need it for new technical words. But I needed it to learn to read in the first place." *But did they?* Beyond learning the basic consonant sounds, how much were they helped by rules of phonics? How much faster might they have learned to read had they been taught mainly by *good* methods of word recognition? Could they have learned all those rules or the most helpful rules *after* they learned to read through third-grade level? (Technical words tend to appear more at fourth grade level, and are more phonetically consistent than the "small" words in the first three grade levels.)

"But the trouble with learning via word recognition," many people think, "is that the child has to memorize a different letter configuration for every word, and that's an *impossible* task." It is not impossible, because every good reader has done exactly that! He or she has memorized thousands of words and word forms and recognizes them instantly. It may be easier, with excellent methods, to memorize words by sight than to memorize all the rules and their variants and exceptions, for the English language is not very phonetically consistent. Vowels are much less consistent than consonants, which is why we recommend that consonant sounds be well learned before reading words (see the research "On Teaching Phonics First" in Adams 1994).

When, How, and How Much Phonics

Researchers disagree on when, how, and how much to teach phonics. They cannot conclusively settle the debate (witness the last 50 years' literature on how to teach reading, including the most recent attempts in Adams 1994, if you have the time). Or, consider my presupposition that the research has been badly flawed.

Often a very large portion of school time is spent learning many, many phonics rules. Some rules help to decode many words. In other cases, several rules are needed in order to decode just a few words. In order to decode a word by phonics, the student has to remember instantly *all* the rules which are needed for a particular word. Phonics rules must therefore be overlearned in order not to slow down the reader.

But how many overlearned phonetic rules will an average student keep on the "front burner" of his or her mind? When decoding consumes reader time, the flow of thought is lost and interest decreases.

The rationale given for the extensive teaching of phonics is that a good reader needs to know hundreds of words, and no developing reader can remember hundreds of words by sight. However, this is exactly what a good reader does—he or she remembers hundreds of words by sight! Good readers with high comprehension are not doing fast continuous decoding, but fast automatic word identification. The mental emphasis is being placed on text meaning.

Whether a reader initially learns words by sight, phonics rules, or a combination of sight and phonics, he or she ultimately transfers into sight identification all words except occasional new ones. Rapid sight identification ability comes from repeatedly seeing the same word with a small enough time gap between sightings to remember that word from the previous sighting. Even most good spellers visualize words without decoding.

It is the thesis of this book that sight reading methods have been under-appreciated and under-explored for teaching reading. I propose that these methods, included in chapter 3, should consume the bulk of time that beginning readers spend their first year. Along with a carefully-sequenced introduction of new words and repetition of new word sightings, the sight methods can be combined with a few selected phonics rules that are easy to learn and easy to apply to many common words (assuming letters and their sounds are learned). Instead of taking the student's time, motivation, and memory storage to learn phonics rules that apply to just a few words, just teach those words by sight. When an initial core of sight words is overlearned, more time can be spent on the most useful and easily-remembered phonics rules.

Once the student begins reading a half hour or more per day, the reading itself teaches and reinforces learning of words faster than exercises can do. A story holds more interest than many exercises.

Most good readers use only a minimum of phonics to decode a new word. They rely more heavily on context. Wilson (1988) states that when good readers encounter words they do not recognize, they first ask what would make sense. When poor readers meet words they do not know, they initially try to sound out words. The following illustration demonstrates why only a minimum of phonics is needed when beginning readers come to a word they do not know:

Suppose a child is stuck on a word in the following sentence (Hammond 1983):

The ___ growled.

If the reader simply guesses, he or she has about one

chance in 25,000 (the number of words he or she might know, counting word forms) of guessing right. If he or she tries phonics, the word may be phonetic, partly phonetic, or nonphonetic. He or she might not remember many rules or even those that apply to this sentence. He or she is likely to remember mainly consonants, if remembering phonics rules at all.

If the student asks, "What word would make *sense?*" He or she then increases chances of getting the word from one in 25,000 to perhaps one in 25. What word makes sense?

pet, cat, puppy, poodle, female, bulldog, dog, collie?

The need for phonics is often limited to knowing consonant sounds when reading for meaning takes priority. In the above example, when meaning is first sought from the context, the student will likely read the word correctly if he or she knows only the consonant sounds. He or she can guess that "d g growled" probably reads "dog." A poor reader, letting his or her mind wander until required to decode the word the teacher points to, might try "dig." The more students read for meaning they less they need to rely on the many phonics rules for a myriad of vowel sounds.

Good readers tend to use the top-down approach more often than bottom-up:

T	↓	semantics (meaning)	P	↑
O	↓		U	↑
P	↓		M	↑
D	↓		O	↑
O	↓	syntax (word arrangement)	T	↑
W	↓		T	↑
N	↓		O	↑
	↓	phonics	B	↑

When semantical and syntax clues are missing, a bottom-up approach is preferred.

Scope, Sequence, and Timing

It is my preference to teach consonant sounds first, then long, and then short vowels. The reason is that if students know what sound (usually a consonant) a word begins with, that sound can be a clue for them to decode the word. The long vowel sounds are easiest to learn, since they are the same as the letters that represent them, although a case could be made for teaching short vowels first, since they have fewer spellings.

Many phonics programs cram the teaching of most phonics rules into the first and second grades. I have carefully weighed recent as well as old approaches and advocate teaching phonics with a time table similar to that of Gunning (1994), who advocates teaching phonics over a period of two or three years. We might stretch that to three or four, for the following reasons:

1. The purpose of phonics is to decode unknown words. This is a fruitful goal when needed for an occasional word; however, learning *many* new words, which needs to be done in first grade, can be taught more efficiently by sight and context. Many phonics rules could be taught in later grades, when students have mastered a core sight vocabulary to which they can compare new words and apply phonics rules.

2. Students encounter more regular words of Latin and Greek origin, with endings such as *-ation, -ous,* or *-ious,* in the third and fourth grades. By this time students could be

more secure and have a good attitude about reading, no longer struggling to recognize a basic sight vocabulary. If they like reading and are up to grade level, they tend to get snagged less, are less overwhelmed, and are more prepared to deal with the more regular word endings and suffixes encountered in longer and more difficult words.

3. The Sounds of O chart illustrated why phonics should be taught "less at first" and stretched over a period of three to four years. The letter O includes only a fraction of phonics rules to be learned.

How to Begin a Reading Program (The "Get 'em Reading First" Philosophy)

The beginning reader should *enjoy* reading. One only enjoys what one succeeds at and what is interesting and only does what one either enjoys or expects to enjoy. How many little children have anticipated joyfully for years that one day they will learn to read, only to be disappointed at how very slowly they do learn, with all kinds of confusion over vowel sounds?

I am an advocate of the "Get 'em Reading First" philosophy. Students should be reading as soon as they begin first grade—just as soon as they know enough letter sounds to read words they understand. Many children expect to learn how to read the first day of school. There are many ways we can fulfill that expectation (see chapter 3, Instant Sight Reading, Whole Passage, and Language Experience).

We can also kill that joy of reading and the expectancy of success with which most children come to school when we bog down reading with too many rules, when we constantly stop the child's reading to make him or her sound out words, when we give too many new words to struggle with, when we give a library book with exciting pictures and a sixth-grade vocabulary he or she cannot read, when we stop to discuss something so often during a story that he or she cannot enjoy "flowing" with the story, and when we do not allow "losing oneself" in reading at the independent level.

The Reason for Having Students Read at Their Independent Level

Students reading at their independent level are reading the material in wholes: whole phrases, whole lines, whole sentences. They do not see separate words but read words by groups, associating words, sentences, or thoughts to comprehend the framework for the whole passage. Comprehension is association-dependent; that is, in order to understand what they are reading, readers must pull together separate words into whole thoughts and then relate those thoughts to the thoughts they will read next.

This association would be impossible unless done at an appropriate rate. Most readers compare text best when they read at a rate similar to normal conversation (100-150 words per minute or faster). Reading one word at a time, with pauses between, makes it nearly impossible to extract information beyond the word. Sentence comprehension takes place in the short-term memory (STM)—but only if *all* the words of the sentence get into the STM at the same time. Martin (1968) showed that a pause of as little as two seconds could lower comprehension. Geough (1972) adds that if it takes too long to read a given word, the content of the immediately preceding words will have been lost from the STM. The child's oral reading will sound like a list because he or she is, in fact, reading a list. On the other hand, fast-paced readers can experience the same problems when reading material that is too difficult for them at a rate that is too fast. The following diagram is one way of illustrating the levels at which students read:

Difficulty Level		*Read by*
Difficult reading	↓	syllables
	↓	separate words
	↓	lines
	↓	sentences
	↓	paragraphs
Very easy reading	↓	able to scan

The following table illustrates one way teachers can provide different amounts of support for students at the various levels of difficulty:

Independent reading level:	minimal support
Instructional level:	moderate support
Frustration level:	full support

If the reader is already fluent and your purpose is to teach him or her to read material that is a little harder or if it is mainly to teach content, then give material at the **instructional** level. Support reading only as much as needed for comprehension. Suggest that the reader plan on rereading at least once before comprehension questions are discussed or problems are worked.

If the reader is already fluent and has a need to read

difficult material or a need to learn how to read difficult material, then teach him or her on an individual basis how to tackle material at the **frustration** level. In frustration-level reading, constantly relate pieces to each other and look for an overall meaning or framework. Other helps at the frustration level include highlighting, glossary-writing, diagramming, mapping, marginal notes, arrows showing relationships, underlining, summarizing, inferring, making question-answer pairs, or reading out loud.

If the reader is not yet fluent, let him or her learn fluency on easy material (at the **independent** level). Let the student practice several rereadings of material on which he or she has demonstrated a high degree of accuracy, so he or she will not be practicing errors while unsupervised. If he or she cannot read without errors, then supervise! Many of the methods in chapter 3 will help you know what to do.

Wholeness and/or Integration

There is much research to support that reading is taught best when students utilize authentic, real-life, familiar words and concepts and when aided by pictures or other contextual clues. The following are three important factors to remember:

Context. Researchers support teaching words in context rather than in isolation. Hammond (1983) suggests that word analysis be taught *after* reading the selection. Although teachers often wish to teach skills, it is more important to the student to understand and hear the whole story—then he or she will be more interested in learning skills.

Personal meaning. High meaning makes words easy to learn, even more than short length or high frequency exposure. This principle explains why the first words students learn are often from daily use—their own names, streets, names of schools or local businesses, family or favorite car, names of games, toys, theaters, restaurants, TV programs, audio or video cassettes, and their parents' names.

Extra hints. A big help to beginning reading is the use of prompts and cues to help the reader looking at a word to make quickly a sensible guess (not a wild guess—wild guessing comes from introducing too much too fast without prompts and cues). Any prompts and cues help beginning readers—the size of the word, the shape of the word, the only long word in the story, the word that fits with the picture, the word printed in red or bold, the word that was discussed before the story was read, the word that always comes after another word, etc. Do not worry that the beginning reader will need the prompt all his or her life. When the student sees the word and recognizes it enough times with a prompt, he or she will not need the prompt any longer, especially if "weaned" from early prompts gradually, much as a parent might wean the child from training wheels on a first bicycle or from water wings after initial swimming lessons. A rule of thumb might be: "Do anything that is legal and moral to help the beginner quickly recognize the word."

Now you know some of the reasons behind what you will be learning in this manual. You are ready to plan the kind of customized reading program you will learn about in the next chapter, and the following chapter will provide the methods you can use in your customized program.

2

Customizing a Personal Reading Program

"Charlie" was a mildly retarded adult who could barely speak in sentences and could not read past first grade level. He stumbled over even the most basic words. One day a teacher sat down at a typewriter and asked him to tell her about the place where he had most enjoyed living. He described a house and woods where he had lived during several happier years of childhood. The teacher typed about 200 words of his own description.

She read it back to him. They discussed it. The teacher then read it *with* Charlie, helping him sweep his fingers smoothly under the lines as he read. After making him a copy, the teacher had Charlie "sweep" his copy while she read hers. After a break, they repeated the last step. The teacher then read a sentence, and Charlie read the same sentence. The teacher read the next sentence, and Charlie read it after her, and so they continued throughout the entire narrative, again and again, faster and faster. Next, they read it together. Finally Charlie was ready to read it by himself,

with the teacher simply telling him any word he did not
recognize. During the tutoring, Charlie could read anything
he repeated often enough and could recognize those same
words in a different story.

Teachers and/or readers who try some of the methods
above (explained in detail in chapter 3) will find that
varying the methods for repeated rereadings quickly builds
vocabulary. The following pages outline a reading program
that can be customized for any reader, with adaptations and
deletions for varied age groups and maturity.

After aiding the tutor in determining the reader's
appropriate independent or instructional reading level, this
chapter briefly explores five areas needing to be addressed
when customizing a reading program. Part I includes
suggestions for emergent readers—for those who are new
to the world of print, especially young children. Part II
outlines the few beginning phonics rules to master before or
in the early stages of reading. Part III shows how to give
readers a "jump start" to quick reading success the first day
of school, which could be emulated at home or in a tutoring
situation, and Part IV demonstrates an overview of word
mastery over three or four years for primary learners, a time
period which would be much shorter for adults. Part V then
suggests one way to implement a complete phonics
program. The rest of the chapter is organized on a more
specific step-by-step chronological schedule one might
follow in carrying out the customized program.

How Do I Select a Book
at the Independent Level?

A true beginner can start with a "wordless" book (the
pictures tell a story, but there are no words: see Wordless
Books, chapter 3). To select a book at a more advanced
reading level, you could, of course, have the student just

begin reading a book. If you find that he does not recognize many of the words, try downscaling levels (try using a graded basal series—see glossary) until you find another book or story in which the learner comfortably knows all but one or two words in a three- to five-minute sitting. The speed should feel comfortable, and the material should be "easy."

There are much more sophisticated methods to select material at a child's independent level (see glossary for an explanation of reading levels): using a readability graph, such as Fry's, a readability computer program (see appendix and chapter 4), or reading inventories (tests) usually found in basal reading programs (see glossary). The easiest method I know of is the Middle-of-the-Book Test (see chapter 3). A good reader or teacher simply asks the poor or beginning reader to read a few paragraphs on a page randomly found in the book or story. If this selection is read fluently without errors, it is likely at independent level. If it is read haltingly with few errors, it may be at the instructional level and can be learned by rereading. (Frustration level reading is addressed in chapter 3). To begin with, the reader should start at a level at which he or she can read with little or few errors. If the initial level chosen is too low, quickly accelerating to higher grade levels will satisfy most readers.

The following outline summarizes a beginning reading program, starting with emergent readers. All parts can be adapted to any age reader.

Bare Bones Outline of a Personalized Reading Program

Part I. Emergent Reading (Preparation for reading)

The purpose of this segment is to teach children to

value reading and books (by reading to the child, modeling reading yourself, picking high-interest material, raising expectations that the child will become a good reader, and providing many positive experiences with printed materials).

A second goal is for students to understand print (by learning automatic and recognition of the alphabet, recognizing letter shape similarities and dissimilarities, learning which direction to hold and read books, and recognizing a few basic everyday words).

Since many books are available on emergent literacy (see glossary, references, and bibliography), parents, teachers, and librarians can readily find many ideas to use with emergent readers.

Part II. Phonics

A study of phonics at this stage consists of learning the appearance and sounds of the consonants to mastery level (fast automatic recognition). Some readers and teachers will likely prefer adding the long and short vowels at the beginning of a reading program (see rationale for teaching phonics in chapter 1).

Adults may need a phonics review, reteaching, or teaching, depending on their phonics background. Refer to chapter 3, Phonics, for a list of the most basic phonics instruction they should learn well. Chapter 4 suggests several phonics workbooks for adults.

Part III. Jump-Start into Reading

This is a quick jump-start into meaningful sentence reading, utilizing strategies from the chapter 3 collection of methods, which are highly specialized for specific purposes and are based on presuppositions about how children learn to read quickly and the "Get 'em Reading First" philosophy (see chapter 1).

Mature Beginning Readers

Basically, any student can begin reading by reading. At the first session, after ascertaining reading level and a quick review (or teaching) of consonant sounds, the tutor can guide the adult reader in a selection of reading material at his or her level. The tutor, after listening to the adult read to determine the independent reading level, can select one of several methods to begin with (see chapter 4, Resources for Adult Beginning Readers). Public adult education or GED centers often offer low-level, high-interest books for adults.

Perhaps the tutor might choose to read the selection through the first time so the adult reader can follow the words and comprehend the overall meaning. Thus, on the first rereading, the reader can relate the words he or she is reading to the meaning of the whole selection. Perhaps the tutor will choose Unison Reading if the adult is afraid, or Paired or Parroted Reading when the student has more confidence. The tutor can follow with the Cloze or Alternate Reading Exercise. Finally, the reader can read through the entire selection, asking the tutor/teacher for words he or she has forgotten. This progression will also work well with children who are slow or struggling readers.

Young Beginning Readers

Teachers can jump-start the beginning reader who often comes to school expecting to learn to read on the first day by using one or more of the following methods described in chapter 3:

Get 'em Reading First
Instant Sight Reading
Read-proofing a Book
Patterned or Predictable Book Reading
Language Experience
One Word at a Time

Whatever methods the teacher chooses, the vocabulary learned one day must be repeated and reinforced daily thereafter. The Instant Sight Reading method lends itself well to a small group or individual and would be more difficult to manage with a large group of students.

Part IV. Building a Vocabulary

The goal of this phase is twofold:

a. *The core vocabulary.* The reader quickly (in the first few days or weeks) builds a basic vocabulary of at least 1000 easily-recognized words to automaticity (see glossary).

b. *A more sophisticated vocabulary.* The reader masters—over a period of months or years—word recognition of all the words good readers generally know by the end of third grade.

It is in Part IV that readers will use most of the methods in chapter 3. Many of the words learned, especially in the core vocabulary (such as those in the Dolch Basic Sight Words and Fry's Instant Words in the appendixes) are nonphonetic and are best taught with the word-recognition methods in chapter 3.

Part V. Learning the "Rest" of Phonics

With consonants already learned under Part I and II and

a fairly large third-grade level vocabulary attained by the end of Part IV, the reader is now ready to learn the phonics rules that will help him or her decode the new words he or she will meet, from fourth-grade level through college and beyond. Many of these longer words, derived from Greek and Latin roots, follow more consistent phonics rules than those of Anglo-Saxon origin. Unusual phonics rules will make more sense when applied to words already learned, and readers will be able recognize similar patterns in other learned and new vocabulary words, including irregular ones. Lists of well-known phonics programs are included in chapter 4.

Examples of Customized Reading Programs

To orient you to how a program might be customized for different types of individuals, several examples follow. Each example includes some elements from Parts II, IV, and V (briefly explained earlier in this chapter).

Example A: Janie

"Janie" was a naughty little girl who was sent home from kindergarten for general disobedience and hurting other children. After obtaining permission, her embarrassed mother dragged Janie along to her own community college adult remedial reading class to "sit it out." While the adults were reading independently, the teacher of the class customized a program for Janie in the following manner: first, she sternly told Janie that if she attended her mother's reading class, she would have to read when the adult learners in the class were started on their own independent reading. Janie replied, "But I cannot read anything." The teacher answered, "You will read those books," pointing to some very simple patterned books for preschoolers.

One sentence and one picture appeared on each page:

I see a horse.
I see a pig.
I see a chick.
I see a cow.

Janie quickly learned to "read" the first book. Of course, her reading was just memorizing and looking at the pictures—but that was a victorious first step.

Pointing out each word, the teacher then taught Janie to sweep her finger under the words as she read them. She was also directed to look at the picture *first* each time she turned the page.

Soon she excitedly read the book to her mother, who was doubtful that this was really reading. But Janie soon mastered the next book.

The farmer rides a horse.
The farmer rides a mule.
The farmer rides a tractor.

Within two hours Janie was reading about 50 words. The teacher copied the sentences for her mother, and Janie retained and practiced her "books" and generalized into other easy books—and did not get kicked out of kindergarten anymore.

Janie already knew most consonant sounds, although she needed review. However, Janie's poor entry attitude toward reading restricted the adult reading teacher from teaching even the preliminary consonant sounds first. They were reinforced later with activities and words she had learned in her books. Once the patterned books were mastered (see Patterned or Predictable Book Reading in chapter 3), Janie began reading some low-level library books and preprimers in a basal series (see glossary). Having experienced success, high-interest, and variety in her reading, she was given more and more advanced materials, including a weekly reader, more library books at her independent level, and a first-grade primer. Her reading was checked orally, and if a story was not mastered to fluency, she was asked to read it again and again, using the Paired, Parroted, and Unison methods in chapter 3. Only when mastery was achieved was she allowed to progress in the basal or to choose another library book.

Example B: Jack

Jack was a fifth-grade boy who was very humiliated in a multigrade classroom because he could not read as well as the first-grade girls. He hated school and was depressed. The teacher was caring but unwilling to depart from rigid guidelines and schedules. A consultant asked the teacher if she would assign a teenage boy to tutor Jack for an hour each evening and two on Sundays, beginning with second-grade books at his independent level. The teacher refused to allow Jack to begin at the second-grade level, assuming that he would be further humiliated by having to read at such a low level. The consultant then arranged to tutor the boy for two hours, with the stipulation that he stay within the fifth-grade reader.

As soon as the consultant took Jack into a separate room, Jack tearfully explained that he could not read a single page in the book and that the consultant may as well not try to help him. Mr. Brown, the consultant, replied, "When we're done today, you'll be able to read a page."

For two hours Mr. Brown alternated tutorial methods of reading with brief outdoor exercise, discussion periods, and snacks. At the end of two hours Jack could read the first two pages in the book well and the rest of the first story with a little struggling.

That first story represented a gain of seventy words in two hours, and Jack's first-ever success at reading. The teacher was convinced and arranged for a tutor to teach Jack a page a night until he caught up. Phonics, too, were dropped until he caught up, except to occasionally reinforce and review beginning sounds in context. Most of the time the teacher merely told Jack the word if he asked for help when reading silently. The rest of the time the teacher used MORE, ARE, Cloze, Unison, and Whole Passage methods from chapter 3.

Example C: Mrs. Miller

Susan Miller achieved and maintained a stable life by sheer willpower. As a single parent of three with no steady income, she was determined to better herself and enrolled in a small college dedicated to helping disadvantaged students achieve academically. Because of her poor reading background, she enrolled in a remedial class.

The teacher listened to each student read, including Susan, the first day. She was put into an adult graded reading series at third-grade level. When Susan came to a word she did not know, she asked the teacher, who told her immediately. At the end of the story, Susan answered comprehension questions and read a few paragraphs with the teacher. After several days of practice on her own with independent reading, she could join the class for a new book. The book, much above Susan Miller's reading level, was called *Obsessive Love*. However, the teacher had written word definitions in the margins of her own book and pretaught the vocabulary for the first chapter (see Vocabulary Drill in chapter 3). First, the class followed along in their books silently as they listened to the teacher read the first chapter. They reread it in unison. Then the teacher used Cloze, leaving off final words of sentences, followed by Parroted Reading. When class members were ready to read the chapter themselves, they sat in groups and asked others the words they did not know. They came up to the teacher's desk to read the most difficult word meanings, which were written in the margins of the teacher's book. Since most of the class identified with the lovers in *Obsessive Love,* they were highly motivated to read the book. They also felt like sophisticated readers, since they were reading their first hardcover adult book.

The adults who practiced reading at least one hour daily saw their vocabularies grow rapidly. Soon the teacher spent one or two days weekly teaching phonics principles and patterns, helping students with spelling and grammar. Students used workbooks for these exercises (see chapter 4 for suggestions). Those who were motivated and practiced faithfully and regularly were rewarded by passing a proficiency test and advancing into regular college classes.

Sample Customized Schedule for Children

The handmade booklet "What Do I Pet?" (see appendix E) provides a sample reading passage for new 6-year-old first-grade beginning readers who know their letters and sounds and who will read it while you follow these steps.

1. *Select a reading passage at the appropriate level.* "What Do I Pet?", though not individualized, is of

appropriate interest for a whole class, small group, or individual. It would be best to duplicate two sets per student on cardstock (one to use at school and one to practice at home). For guidance in selecting your own materials, see Independent Reading, Middle-of-the-Book Test, Basal Readers, and Categorizing Books, chapter 3, and How Do I Select a Book at the Independent Level? at the beginning of this chapter. If the reader has had no phonics instruction (does not know beginning consonant sounds or letters), include that instruction either before or simultaneously with the other methods for new readers (see Phonics, chapter 3). To find appropriate reading material, use the resources in chapter 4. Once the reading level is confirmed, the following methods from chapter 3 would be appropriate to look over and have in mind to use as you read the rest of this chapter.

For a student who has never read anything:
Get 'em Reading First	Phonics
Instant Sight Reading	Language Experience
Patterned or Predictable	Whole Passage
Book Reading	Prompts and Cues
Core Vocabulary	

For a students at the lowest reading levels:
All of the above methods	Basal Readers
Paired Reading	Parroted Reading
MORE	ARE and ARE Cloze
Read-proofing a Book	Rereading

2. *Read the selection the first time through.* As students read along silently and/or look at the pictures, the teacher reads to them aloud.

3. *Discuss briefly the passage being read.* Using "What Do
   I Pet?", you could explore animals the children pet, and
   then those they look at but do not pet.

4. *Use a reading routine.* The instructor explains the
   following routine, using a sweeping motion with his or
   her fingers under the words to be read:

   a. Turn the page
   b. Look at the picture
   c. Read the text (Teacher reads it first time through
      using a sweeping motion under phrases)

   With practice, the teacher can shorten the routine to
   "Turn;" "Look;" "Read."

5. *Have the students reread the selection.* After the teacher
   instructs, "Turn the page" (pause); "Look at the picture"
   (pause); "Read," the group reads in unison with the
   teacher, who checks whether the children are studying
   the picture, using the sweeping motion to focus on the
   words, etc.

6. *Have students reread many times.* For other readings on
   the same or other days, tutors can select rereading
   routines from Rereading and Whole Passage methods in
   chapter 3. Depending on student age, maturity, attention
   span, and experience, rereading for mastery should be
   done a minimum of three times per selection over a
   period of one hour to two or three days. Some students
   will need more practice than others, and some will be
   able to complete rereading tasks faster than others.
   The following are examples:

a. Use the Parroting method, remembering to sweep fingers over the words in each line.

b. When the student can read a whole section well by Parroting, have him or her read the selection using the Cloze method.

c. When he or she can read it well using the Cloze method, have him or her read the passage again using other methods, such as the Paired Reading method.

d. Then have him or her read the passage alone.

Remember not to go on to the next sentence, paragraph, or page until the student has mastered the first sentence, paragraph, or page. Do not go on to a different book until the first book is mastered. Continue to review the first book on occasion, even after the next book has been started.

6. *Make connections between the passage and the students' own world.* Students may color the pictures and add flower stickers. Other creative ideas might include bringing a pet rabbit for everyone to pet.

7. *Encourage students to practice at home.* After the passage is mastered, send a copy of the passage/text home with the student. If the student is a young child, you might include a note to parents suggesting they have their child read the selection to as many different individuals as possible, to encourage rereading variety.

Sample Customized Steps for Adults

The following steps will be applicable to an adult at first-grade reading level.

1. *Select a high-interest, short passage.* Seated at a computer or typewriter, the tutor asks the student to tell him or her one of the happiest times of his life. Type everything he says in complete sentences, with double spacing and dividing the selection into short 3-4 sentence paragraphs, until a page is completed. Keep sentence structure and words simple, based on the student's reading level and learning potential (see Language Experience in chapter 3). Make several copies.

2. *Select one paragraph for mastery.* Using the Whole Passage method in chapter 3, point out distinctive characteristics of certain words (See Phonics and Vocabulary Drill in chapter 3). If the adult enjoys it, you can adapt the Instant Sight Reading techniques (chapter 3) to the typed paragraph, making four sets of sentence strips of the passage: one for sentences, one for individual words that can be rearranged, and an identical pair of whole sentence strips and word strips for the student to take home for practice.

3. *Encourage the student to practice at home.* After the student masters the small selection (in one sitting), send it home with him or her for practice.

It might be a good idea now to skim chapter 3, just to

get an idea of the various methods and tips available to you. In the future, chapter 3 will be a handy, alphabetized reference of methods to adapt to varying circumstances.

3

Suggested Methods for Building Fluency

A reading teacher once visited a second-grade classroom where few students could read anything. The classroom teacher, Mrs. Hazel, was frustrated by low reading levels, by "such short attention spans" during silent sustained reading of library books, and by the failure of the students to apply phonics rules to their reading. Mrs. Hazel was using a combination of whole language and thematic instruction, not graduated textbooks.

With only two months to go before the year's end, the reading teacher gave Mrs. Hazel a drastic plan. First she asked her to put all her library books in the middle of the floor. "Box up all the books that no one can read easily." She did. Few were left. "Now put yellow tape on the books that your best readers can read independently, and put matching yellow tape inside the desks of your best readers." She did. "Put red tape on the easiest books and matching red tape inside the desks of the rest of your students." After

Mrs. Hazel did this she brought in a stack of old first-grade readers and put red tape on them, too.

The reading teacher loaned Mrs. Hazel boxes of high-interest low-vocabulary, first- and second-grade books. She then asked the teacher to read her students these books during story time instead of the "good literature" books that none of her students could hope to read. Mrs. Hazel put pages from the borrowed books on the overhead projector, so her students could read in unison with her. Sometimes Mrs. Hazel asked those with blue eyes to read a paragraph, and sometimes she asked those without blue eyes. Sometimes students who wore something red finished the sentence Mrs. Hazel was reading, and sometimes it was finished by those who were not wearing something red. Mrs. Hazel spent some hours recording stories on a tape recorder for students who needed more vocabulary reinforcement than she could give them herself. By the end of the year most of those students were up to grade level, and she could spend story-reading time introducing the "good literature" of high interest and slightly higher vocabulary levels.

Chapter 3 alphabetically lists the kinds of methods mentioned above so that you can plan powerful reading programs and strategies for yourself, your child, your student, or, if you are a librarian, ways to help teachers and beginning readers find appropriate reading selections at the appropriate level.

"How-tos" are explained first under Method, followed by the reason or Rationale for the method. You might want to browse through the entire chapter, earmarking for future reference methods that appear useful.

Activity-Based Reading

Method

After the student (or teacher) reads a short selection or part of a longer selection, design an activity, possibly planned with the student, that develops one or more of the concepts just read. If students read *If You Give a Mouse a Cookie,* they might bake and/or eat cookies after the reading. After reading about monster trucks, take students to a truck dealership to see one or find one in an on-line encyclopedia. Activities can be long or short, depending on the outcome desired. Rereadings can follow the activity.

High school students, after reading about the Civil War, will be stimulated by a tape from the video series, *The Blue and the Gray.* Computer software programs are excellent activities for any age. A discussion, a visitor who is an expert, a field trip, or a "break" doing something different can freshen the appetite for reading. Activities can take place before, after, or between readings.

Rationale

This method is designed for students who dislike or hate reading or who dislike sitting still for any length of time. It can be adapted to any age reader and can energize active students whose interest or attention span may be waning (see "Hate" Reading and One Word at a Time).

Alternate Reading Exercise (ARE)

Method

The tutor reads the first sentence, and the student reads the next. The process is repeated until the passage is read.

A variation of ARE, the ARE Cloze (see next section), is much like the written and oral Cloze methods (not included in this book) which are used largely for comprehension.

Rationale

This method works best with *short* passages, such as a paragraph, page, or very short story. Reading alternately provides the student with comprehension support, because he or she hears the next sentence after the material just read, and a focus of attention on the text, since he or she must read the next sentence. After the reader is comfortable with the routine, the length of passages read can be extended.

ARE Cloze (Cloze)

Method

The teacher or parent reads all but the last word, phrase, or portion of a sentence. The student finishes the sentence or phrase, and the leader starts another sentence, as follows:

Teacher: "The boy rode his motorcycle all the way—"
Student: "home."

Teacher: "As he turned into his driveway, a large, puffy object—"

Student: "caught his attention."

The student must be coached to finish the phrase or sentence as rapidly as possible in order not to slow down the pace.

Rationale

This method is not used until the student is familiar with the vocabulary in the passage. It is not usually used on a first reading but is used as a part of rereading, often in combination with the whole passage method. ARE (Alternate Reading Exercise) Cloze gives the student the support of reading the prior words, aiding comprehension of the portion he or she will read. The leader reads as much or as little as he or she feels the student needs to successfully finish the sentence or phrase. In order for the student to keep up the pace, he or she must read with the leader, thus practicing fluent reading.

Basal Readers

Method

Basals, or books that are part of a graded set that has carefully sequenced, incremental vocabulary development, are frequently used for an elementary school reading program. Students start out with the preprimers, or books with just one or two words on the first page. Succeeding pages reuse the same words with different pictures, gradually adding one or two new words every few pages, until (by the end of the book) the student has learned approximately 15-25 words. The student then graduates into the next level, where more words are added. Teachers should supplement basal reading with rereading and library books to reinforce word sightings. Children need more exposure to words than one reading alone can give.

Rationale

Basals follow the principles of how words are recognized: using words already meaningfully used in the reader's spoken language, new words are introduced visually, aurally, and understandably. They are then read over and over in context within a short enough time so the word is not forgotten between "sightings." The number of times it needs to be resighted depends on the individual student. If students reread their stories for additional sightings within a short enough time frame, new words are well-learned before other words are added.

Categorizing Books

Method

There are many ways to categorize books, but this is a very simple way for busy teachers and parents to help beginning readers categorize their own books.

First, separate all the books in your library that are too hard for anyone in your room to read. Do not make these available until you have readers who can read them. Second, sort the rest into three sections (or however many you wish): (a) those that can be read independently by your advanced readers, (b) those that can be read independently by your slowest readers, and (c) those that most of the rest of your readers can read. Third, mark each of these books on the spine with colored tape or dot labels: (a) red on the easiest books, (b) blue on the hardest books, and (c) yellow on the rest. Finally, color-code a designated spot on the *inside* of your readers' desks with matching tape or dot label, according to their reading levels.

Rationale

Much research has disclosed that students do not make good use of their time during silent, sustained reading when they do not read at their independent reading level. In order to build fluency, students must read at their independent level. Categorizing books makes choosing easier for students—they may choose their own books, but only within a certain level that will guarantee successful silent reading.

Comprehension

Method

Although comprehension is integral to fluency, an artificial separation has been made in order to emphasize sight methods which build fluency. A few methods are introduced here, however, because they are helpful and integral to fluent reading.

The most basic comprehension strategy to enhance automaticity is to choose subject matter readers are familiar with. When choosing less familiar material because of its educational or high interest value, however, it is important for students to understand and be oriented to what they will read: curiosity will be heightened and anxiety will be lessened. Asking predictive, open-ended, high-order thinking questions and eliciting what students already know about a subject are common ways to ignite interest: "What do you think will happen? Why? Do you know anyone with leukemia? What are the symptoms like? Is there a cure?"

Giving a purpose for reading and reviewing and explaining only the essential vocabulary before reading are common *prereading* activities. Giving a student reflective questions to think about while he or she reads is a *during reading* activity. Most students like reading a selection, if it is not too long, all the way through without interruption. They often do not like being interrupted by teachers for discussion or for making more predictions. When the reading is finished, students need to be debriefed. They have issues that need clarification, and many questions are cleared up during the *postreading* discussion. Many of these questions, however, can be answered by rereading, if the leader is skillful in leaving for the student that which he or she can do for him or herself.

Rationale

Readers need guidance in interpreting new material. Involving students in the prereading activities above develops and activates background and experience, thus enhancing comprehension. Leaving most vocabulary for the reader to learn on his or her own gives the student the joy of learning new words from context clues. If the only long word on a page is "parachute," and there is a picture of a parachute on the opposite page, let the reader experience the thrill of figuring out a long, nonphonetic word from context.

Since the emphasis of this manual is on fluency, many other strategies that build comprehension are not included here, but tutors are encouraged to explore the additional selections listed in chapter 4, references, and bibliography.

Core Vocabulary

Method

A list of 500 high-frequency words drawn from school materials make up about 80% of the words students in grades 3–9 will use in school. Of these, ten words (the, of, and, a, to, in, is, you, that, it) comprise more than 20% of the words that beginners will see in books at their level (Gunning 1994). We first teach these words in context but isolate them to study their form (i.e., write them on flash cards or on the board). Almost any of the methods in this chapter are helpful in building this common core vocabulary (see Prompts and Cues, Instant Sight Reading, Patterned or Predictable Book Reading, Word Attack, or Vocabulary Drill for methods of building a core vocabulary; and Dolch Basic Sight Words and Fry's Instant Words in the appendixes for sample core vocabularies).

After a core vocabulary is acquired, near the end of third grade level, students are able to read a wide variety of library books.

Rationale

A core vocabulary can range from a few words common to his or her own world which the student reads the first day, to the 500 core words that are common to most school texts through grade nine. If students master these words first, they have an easier time adding uncommon and subject specialized words that require a glossary, dictionary, slow reading, and/or rereading.

Drop Everything and Read (DEAR)

See Sustained Silent Reading (SSR).

Experience

See Language Experience.

Frustration Level

Method

Begin with a short passage that is highly interesting though difficult (usually the reader will preselect meaningful material). Show the reader how to use the dictionary or electronic spell checker to pronounce and understand unknown words. Teach him or her to read and/or reread the previous and/or following sentence(s) to pick up a word's meaning from the context. Teach the student to keep track of meaning with diagrams, arrow notes (i.e., between the word and its appositional definition), little drawings, or summarizations. Sometimes the student will need to go over and over the same sentence. Sometimes he or she should forge ahead and then go back to the frustrating sentence.

In frustration level reading, constantly relate pieces to each other and look for an overall meaning or framework.

A variation has the teacher or parent read the material to the student as the student manually acts out the steps or rephrases what was just read.

Rationale

Occasionally a reader wants to read a manual, text, or selection that is fairly difficult and perhaps beyond his or her vocabulary knowledge or reading ability. If the reader is already fluent and has a need to read difficult material, the above methods are useful tools. If the reader is not fluent, you may wish to read the selection aloud. If the reader insists on reading it him or herself, pre-teach some of the words and assign only one or two sentences, with the student rereading them until they are understood sufficiently to go on.

To ensure success, it is important that a good reader coach or support the student in his or her endeavor.

Get 'em Reading First

Method

This is more a philosophy than a method. Most children come to school *wanting to read*—in fact, many assume they will either learn to read or at least start reading the first day. To avoid discouragement or disillusionment the teacher can give each child a successful reading experience the first day by having each learn a few meaningful words to read to their parents at home. More words learned and overlearned on successive days can provide a core word vocabulary from which to teach phonetic sounds, writing, and reading (see Instant Sight Reading, Language Experience, Patterned or Predictable Book Reading, and Whole Passage for methods that enable children to read on the first day of school).

Rationale

Children expect to learn how to read on the first day of school. It does not matter how few words or whether they are memorized rather than read—a child feels successful if he or she can go home and "read" a selection, however short, to significant others.

"Hate" Reading: What to Do When Students Hate Reading

Method

There are two categories of students who hate reading:

1. *Those who can read.* These students can usually be satisfied if material is found on a subject of interest. This simple solution can become more complex if the student's preoccupations are not easily found in materials at his or her level. To solve this problem, see Read-proofing a Book and Simplifying a Book (in this chapter) and refer to an article called Sustained Silent Reading (Myers and Oliphant 1994).

2. *Those who read poorly or not at all.* Use the same strategies outlined in the paragraph above, but be sure the student reads at a very easy level, perhaps below his or her independent level. The goal is to select materials that utilize words most familiar to the student—those which he or she routinely hears, speaks, thinks, and likes. Use prereading vocabulary drills; offer short-term extrinsic rewards, and remove pressures in non-reading areas such as difficult subjects, clean-up duties, or homework. Try reading alternating with exercise (see Activity-Based Reading). Use rereading or short passages for overlearning so the student experiences a feeling of mastery. Although comprehension can be developed by a postreading discussion, it should be informal. Readers who hate reading tend to dislike a formal question-and-answer format—for them it often feels "fake." Let "artists" show comprehension by creating a picture or poster. (Also see High-Interest Books, High External Rewards, Newspaper Reading, and One Word at a Time.)

Rationale

Students who hate reading usually do so because they have had little success or have been conditioned to dislike reading by being assigned dull workbook pages, being subjected to long rounds of uninteresting comprehension questions, enduring over correction by well-meaning parents or teachers, being forced to read unrehearsed material in the presence of critical peers, or being assigned reading selections that are not a part of their culture, world, or interests. Teachers must overcome built-in resistance that is usually not present in first graders, who approach reading with unbiased anticipation.

If a student hates reading, the primary goal should be for the student to *like* reading. Second, they need to get "over the hump," up to grade level, and successful. Many reading experiences with high-interest books and high success (achievement, advancement) will maximize attainment of these goals.

High External Rewards

Method

Although many teachers make use of rewards, this reward must be special enough to achieve drastic results.

1.   Purchase something very appealing to a maximum of two students, such as matchbox-sized trucks or cars or doll house furniture. Use the items as bait for having students read by either telling them about or showing them *one* of the items.

2.   Using a combination of language experience and instant sight reading (sentence strip) methods, ask the students, one at a time, while the other listens, what kind of car he or she has at home and make a very simple story about cars or trucks (or the rooms of furniture at home) by writing the sentence(s) on sentence strips.

3.   Just as quickly as you can get the first sentence on a strip, ask the student who chose some of the words to read it.

4. Ask the other student to "test" the first student's reading by telling him or her if the reading was correct or by correcting a misread word.

5. If the student read correctly, he or she gets a toy immediately to put in his or her bag.

6. Ask the second student to read the sentence.

7. Ask the second student to reread while the first student checks for correctness.

8. Reward the second student with a toy.

9. Make duplicate sentence strips for each student while they play with their toys. Cut these into word strips and mix up each student's own sentence.

10. Have them rearrange the words correctly and read their sentences.

11. Have them rearrange the words differently (no matter how silly) and reread their new sentences.

12. Have them check each other's readings.

13. Ask the first student to read the second student's sentence, and visa versa, each checking the other's rereading, as above.

14. If they have read correctly so far, reward each with another toy.

15.   Add another new sentence as in steps 2–14, rewarding only after step 14, after both have read their own and each other's old and new sentences.

16.   Repeat the above steps, rewarding as sparingly as possible.

17.   Take a break when necessary. During the break, copy the sentences onto a sheet of primary-lined paper.

18.   Review after the break by reading the "page."

19.   Add another sentence, being sure to use connecting words like "where," "that," or "to."

20.   This can be continued in a tutoring setting after school until the children have mastered 35–40 words between their two stories.

21.   Staple the stories between construction paper and make two copies of each, one for home and one for school.

22.   Send one copy home with instructions for the child to reread the stories to everyone in the family and neighborhood, including cousins, telemarketers, tax collectors, social workers, dogs, and cats, if necessary. Include a note of how well the child did and the importance of rereading. Be sure to explain that the cars or trucks were rewards.

23.   Include a signature page for ten signatures (to ensure ten rereadings).

24.   Be sure to keep the rewards in a special, locked drawer until the child leaves for home. Often very young children will give away their rewards, underestimating their value or badly needing friends. They will also play with them during school hours.

Rationale

Ordinarily we want to teach students to read quickly enough at a high enough interest level to ensure that reading will be its own reward. High External Reward is for rather desperate circumstances in which you need to show a very disheartened student that he or she can read when really trying, or when you might want to test how fast a student could learn if he or she really wanted to.

This method has worked on young children who were considered by their teachers to be "hopeless" and "incorrigible".

High Interest Books

Method

This simple method consists of choosing or helping a student choose a book that appeals to his or her individual interest, such as a book about crabs for a naturalist.

A second application is to choose books for the reader's library that are of interest to anyone because they usually have a captivating plot, a bit of intrigue, or a surprise ending. A story about a little duck (riding on top of a truck) who saved townspeople's lives by honking when the truck's horn refused to function has a plot and a surprise ending

(Kessler 1961). By contrast, a book that shows pictures of ducks and other animals talking to each other at the pond is not as interesting. Especially beautiful or detailed illustrations appeal to some readers, but unless the message or story is equally engrossing, many may not pick it up again (see Read-proofing a Book and Simplifying a Book).

Rationale

This method is a necessity for students who hate reading. When reading is extra hard work, students are not likely to pick up a book that is of low or average interest; on the other hand, they might read eagerly if the selection holds high personal meaning.

Independent Reading Level

Method

When readers recognize about 98% of the words, they have reached their independent level (see glossary). They need little or no support. There are various ways to find a student's independent level; see Middle-of-the-Book Test in this chapter. More formal tests are available in the Teacher's Guides of basal readers. When having a student read a passage, observe whether many words are new or unfamiliar. If there are many, back up to an easier text. If easier texts are still full of new or hesitantly-read words, read just one sentence. You may have to use very beginning reading methods, such as the Instant Sight Reading method, which utilizes sentence strips, and One Word at a Time.

Rationale

Fluency is supported most efficiently by reading at the independent level.

Instant Sight Reading

Method

1. Make a set of verb flash cards for each student. Use a yellow sentence strip (color-coded for verbs—sentence strips are 3" x 24" strips of wide, primary-lined cardstock, available at teaching supply stores). Cut each strip to the length of the word, like a flash card. Use verbs the student is familiar with, such as *telephoned, drove, ate, helped, played, walked, saw, said, were, was, thought, came, has, bring, brought.*

2. Make, or have an assistant make, another set—students take home individual cards as they are learned in school. Students can practice with relatives without fear that the materials will not return to school the next morning.

3. Put a tiny illustrative picture or sticker by each word. The picture does not have to match the meaning perfectly—it is mainly a visual cue.

4. Write the child's initials above each word, in very small letters, for lost-and-found purposes.

5.   Work with one child at a time while other children
     are busy doing other things. Take the word
     telephoned and ask, "Who uses the telephone in
     your house? Whom does Mommy call?" On a blue
     sentence strip (color-coded for nouns and pronouns),
     write his or her answer (e.g., *Daddy*). Also write
     Mommy on a blue sentence strip.

6.   Now the child can put together his first
     "personalized" sentence with three cards:

     Mommy telephoned Daddy.

     Further questions elicit more information, and more
     blue cards are written. Now the child can "mix and
     match" words he or she can read.

     Mommy telephoned Daddy.
     Daddy telephoned Mommy.
     Helen telephoned Mommy.
     Helen telephoned Grandma.
     Mommy telephoned the store.
     Daddy telephoned the office.

7.   Next lesson: add the words *about, a,* and *an.* Choose
     colored cards for the new parts of speech. Now you
     have sentences like:

     Mommy telephoned Grandma about the baby.
     Mommy telephoned Daddy about slippery roads.

8.   Gradually add vocabulary words and let the child
     spread them out wherever there is plenty of space.

The child will be proud of instantly reading "long sentences."

9. Print or type the child's sentences for desk practice and wean him or her from the strong sticker and card color cues.

10. Make language experience charts and personal stories and have the child illustrate them with drawings. Have stencils available for the most common objects (see the Language Experience method).

Rationale

This method is used for the first day, few days, or week of school to meet the expectation beginning readers have of learning how to read the first day of school. Using words they already know and use ensures a high success rate for learning new words. Students can go home armed with cards to show relatives their new words, which can consequently be used to teach new sounds (see the Get 'em Reading First method).

Instructional Level

Method

At the instructional level, when students know approximately 93–95% of the vocabulary of a selection (compared to 98-100% at the independent level), there are many ways to give students the support they need to read with comprehension. Care must be exercised, however, to allow readers the pleasure of discovering as many new words as possible on their own. For example, if the story is about a monkey in a space rocket who returns to earth in a parachute, prereading discussion can focus on predicting how the monkey might land without drilling students on the word "parachute". Pictures, context, word size, and initial letter sound will enable the reader to decode the word.

Support at the instructional level might involve asking what students know about the subject before reading the selection, or it might include clarifying misunderstandings in postreading discussions. Other suggestions are listed under Comprehension, Read-proofing a Book, Vocabulary Drill, Word Attack, and Whole Passage.

Rationale

Although instructional level reading does not build fluency, rereading at that level does. It is important to understand the purposes of the three main reading levels: reading at the *independent level* provides practice for fluent, automatic reading; reading at the *instructional level* stretches the reader's vocabulary in a milieu of familiar words, and *frustration-level* reading, understood to be too difficult, is only used for specific purposes (see Independent and Frustration Levels in this chapter).

Language Experience

Method

The student who cannot write or type tells you an experience he or she has had. Often the experience is one the student has just had with you, such as a trip to the zoo or to the local canning factory. Print or use large type to write the words as the child tells them, using his or her vocabulary. Create a large booklet that can be reread each day. Then use Unison, Paired, Parroted, Cloze, and other reading methods to read and reread the experience.

Rationale

Students learn vocabulary quickly by reading stories or experiences that have high meaning and are comprised of words from their own vocabulary. High interest and high meaning insure high success.

Middle-of-the-Book Test

Method

The teacher or parent listens to the student read a randomly-picked paragraph or page in the middle or last portion of the story, where new vocabulary words are apt to be repeated more frequently than at the beginning where they were incrementally introduced. The teacher diagnoses whether or not the story is to be read or reread, depending on how fluently the student reads the passage.

This method can, and indeed should, be used every time beginning readers wish to check out a book from the library for silent sustained reading or to progress to a new story or book in whatever reading program is being used.

Rationale

This method has been called a cure-all for busy

teachers. If used *before* the student reads the story, it is a quick way to prevent him or her from experiencing failure when attempting text that is too difficult and thus acquiring bad habits such as substituting and deleting words from the text (see also Categorizing Books). If used *after* the student has read the story the required number of times, the Middle-of-the-Book Test is an index of the degree of vocabulary mastery. Although coding miscues in reading, using reading inventories, and categorizing books by readability estimators are reliable when finding out whether students are able to read certain books, they are not always available. The Middle-of-the-Book Test offers a cogent compromise between professional assessment and no assessment at all.

Modeled Oral Reading Exercise (MORE)

Method

The leader models the reading of a sentence in the text exactly as he or she wants it read by the students. The students mimic this intonation and expression. Length of segments varies with difficulty of reading material. Lengthening segments to be read actually gives students more opportunities to read the text.

This method can be used chorally with a whole class, small groups, or individuals.

Rationale

Students learn to make the text meaningful with their voices, developing their concept of how to read on their own. It makes no difference whether they are reading or parroting back what they have just heard. This method works well at instructional or even frustration levels, but at the independent level it is an effective diagnostic tool for problem readers. The errors they make (with the appropriate length of segment) truly reflect which words they have problems identifying (Wilson 1988).

New Word Attack

See Word Attack and Phonics.

Newspaper Reading

Method

Newspapers are good high-interest sources for reading. For older students, use *USA Today,* which has an elementary vocabulary, or *News for You* (see chapter 4). There are also many beginning-level newspapers and periodicals to choose from (see chapter 4). The list of ideas and methods for using newspapers is endless. Here are a few.

Hand out a newspaper or page of a newspaper. Ask students first to read an article they are not going to report on and then to read twice an article they will report on. Have them report to the group.

Some students may prefer newspapers during independent reading time.

Choose an article students may be interested in. Introduce and explain words they may not be able to decode or understand from the context, and ask if anyone knows anything about the subject the article is about, such as a new treatment for leukemia. Read the article while students follow along, and then ask them to read it with you in unison. Use Paired, Parroted, Cloze, and other methods of your choosing for rereading. Discuss the material and ask comprehension questions at the end of the session.

Many prereading activities can be used with newspapers. If you purchase two identical papers, students can learn letter-sound recognition and word discrimination by matching words, letters, paragraphs, and pictures. For example, ask preschoolers to match all the beginning "s" words you have cut out from one newspaper by placing them on top of their mates in another paper. Using smaller or longer words would increase the difficulty level of this activity.

Rationale

Newspapers elicit high interest and provide small segments that will not discourage slow readers who generally dislike lengthy selections. They are helpful for students who already "hate reading" because there are a variety of topics and interest categories to choose from. The prereading activities suggested above will give prereaders help in understanding print.

One Word at a Time

Method

1. *Choose a word.* One word that has special meaning is

chosen for the student to learn, such as "zoo," or perhaps a more customized word, such as the name of the student's dog.

2. *Illustrate the word.* This method works best in a setting, theme, context, or experience. If the student has no or little experience with the word (i.e., has not gone to the zoo or does not have a pet), the tutor arranges for students to have an activity applying that word. The tutor can also read to the student books or articles which illustrate the word or the theme, enriching the student's conceptual understanding.

3. *Give the student a book utilizing that word.* Make a book (see appendix F) which introduces and uses that word either alone or with other familiar words. The word is repeated on several pages, not adding another new word until the sequel or after several pages. When the second word is added, it might be a derivative, if the teacher wants the student to focus on a letter sound (such as "s" in zoos); an article, a number, or another word easily associated with that word (*the* zoo, *one* zoo, *animal* zoo, and zoo *animal*).

Although the pages of the book have a one-word focus, they each have a picture which tells a story or adds new meaning to the word; i.e., if the word is Bill, Bill might be doing something different in each picture. After several pages, the text underneath Bill looking at himself in a mirror might say, "Two Bills."

This method can be combined with other methods, such as Simplifying a Book, Scripted Reading, Alternate Reading

Exercise, ARE Cloze, Activity-Based Reading, "Hate" Reading, and others.

Rationale

Children need many prereading experiences, such as visiting interesting places, being read to, and taking part in discussions about educational topics. The method above is for immature or very young students who have never read before or who have had few or none of these emergent reading experiences. On the contrary, these children may spend much of their time in front of the TV or playing aimlessly, without purpose, planning, or self-discipline. They may get restless listening to a teacher or concentrating on written material.

The principle is to introduce in context only words the student understands at a pace and frequency that will assure mastery.

Oral Reading

Method

Different variations include:

1. Read to the child, who reads along silently.

2. Read with the student in unison.

3. Reader reads to you or to someone else.

4. Reread with expression.

5. SURE: Student's Unassisted Reading Exercise, in which a student reads a rehearsed story at his or her independent reading level to other listening students.

6. TOORE: Teacher-Orchestrated Oral Reading Exercise, in which the class is divided into subgroups. The whole class participates, but each subgroup is unaware of when it will be signaled (hand, bell, or pointing) to start or stop reading. Whenever the bell rings, students are to look up from their reading.

7. Other methods of Oral Reading include:

> Alternate Reading Exercise
> ARE Cloze
> Cloze
> Modeled Oral Reading Exercise
> Paired Reading
> Parroted Reading
> Reader's Theater
> Scripted Reading
> Unison
> Whole Passage

Readers learn how to intonate by silently reading several words ahead. Students can give proper intonation to words if they have heard good modeled reading and have practiced and understand what they are reading.

Rationale

Oral reading is an art that has been largely lost in the United States. Round Robin Reading (asking each child to read orally in turn) has soured many teachers on oral reading because it has embarrassed so many readers. One way to avoid student embarrassment over not being able to read well in front of peers is to use different methods, such as Scripted Reading, or Reader's Theater, and have different purposes for oral reading, such as learning to read with expression. Ideally, teachers should listen daily to students reading selections orally to check for fluency. Used with the Middle-of-the Book Test, oral reading can prevent students from reading selections that are too difficult or from skipping to the next story in a basal reader without having learned the prerequisite vocabulary in the preceding story.

Oral reading is one way to test students' reading. If reading does not flow naturally and fluently, a teacher is able quickly to correct the problem by assigning rereading or by modeling fluent reading. Many adults who have not practiced oral reading shy away from reading aloud in public contexts, such as in church or in other meetings. Purposes for oral reading include (1) modeling good reading, (2) helping a student concentrate and follow reading, (3) supporting comprehension (when the text is difficult), (4) building speed from a slow pace and (5) sparking interest (thus affecting the student's love for reading) with the use of intonation, as when parents and teachers read animatedly to their children (Wilson 1988). One final very important use for oral reading is substituting it for silent reading if the latter reinforces poor reading habits (such as substituting or making up words in the text).

Paired Reading

Method

1. The reader chooses a book from those preselected as

suiting his or her independent or instructional level (at which he or she knows approximately 95%+ of the words).

2. The reader and tutor discuss the book (before and during reading, as needed for comprehension).

3. Both the reader and tutor read and reread the passage out loud together.

4. If the reader makes an error, the tutor repeats the word until the reader reads it correctly.

5. When the text becomes easy enough or has been repeated enough times, the reader makes a prearranged nonverbal signal (knock, nudge, squeeze, etc.) to tell the tutor to be silent. The reader reads alone until an error is made.

6. The tutor uses the same correction procedure, and the two read together again until the reader signals that he or she wishes to read alone.

7. Throughout the process, the tutor praises for correct reading, correction, and signaling to read alone.

8. Readers may try a word they do not know for five seconds before the guide repeats the word, thus limiting reader anxiety.

Rationale

Research shows that parents who use this technique with their children raise their children's accuracy, expressiveness, and fluency (Topping 1989). Although the original researchers advocate children selecting material at any level of difficulty, beginning readers need limits, or they become easily discouraged. However, there is no reason why, if they are very anxious to read something at their frustration level, that they cannot try to do so; however, in that case, the tutor could select one or two sentences to be read and reread for mastery. Much of the rest could be read to the reader. For suggestions on teaching how to read at this level, see Frustration Level in this chapter.

During reading together, the reader receives a model and continuous prompt for good reading. Students practice reading independently as they are able, after having read the selection several times (if needed). Praise reinforces correct reading habits and abilities. Free choice heightens interest, and the intent five-second wait before repeating words limits anxiety (not waiting too long to correct, but giving the reader a chance to attack the word). This method was first promoted for use by parents with their children, but it would be excellent for any beginning reader.

Parroted Reading

Method

1. The reader examines pictures or tables first before reading each page.

2. The tutor reads one sentence at a time, sweeping his or her fingers underneath the words in a smooth motion while reading.

3. The reader repeats the sentence (parrots what the tutor just said) or reads in unison while the tutor sweeps his or her fingers under the words (later the reader can do the sweeping motion him or herself).

This technique can be combined or alternated with Paired Reading. To maximize actual reading, as opposed to merely mimicking what the tutor has just read, the sentences may be lengthened beyond what can be held in the short term memory.

Rationale

This technique models fluent reading while giving the reader autonomous practice immediately after the modeling. It lends more support to the reader than ARE (Alternate Reading Exercise). It is another variation of rereading that provides practice with maximum support. The emphasis is on word recognition and fluency, rather than on expression, as in MORE (see Modeled Oral Reading Exercise). However, parroted reading can overlap with MORE by using MORE for the final reading.

The sweeping motion under the words is important, helping the reader focus on the words at a smoother and perhaps faster pace than he or she might maintain if reading without directing his or her eyes to the words.

Patterned or Predictable Book Reading

Method

Patterned or predictable books are books that repeat

words in the same sequence for easy memorization of vocabulary. The pattern can be a song, as in *Mary Wore a Red Dress* (red dress, red dress); a poem, such as "Mary Had a Little Lamb"; or a sequenced rhyme such as "his is the House that Jack Built" or "Old MacDonald had a Farm," with new words being added to words already learned.

Patterned books vary in degree of repetition, some having only a refrain or phrase that is repeated, while others repeat all words but one. Early readers enjoy starting with the latter; more experienced readers may appreciate the repetitive lyrics of songs or poetry.

Patterned, predictable books are easy to make, especially with software programs like Make-a-Book (see chapter 4 and appendix F). Most readers can learn to write and illustrate their own patterns, which can be as simple as the following:

Sara likes to ride in a car.
Sara likes to ride in a boat.
Sara likes to ride on a train.
Sara likes to ride in an airplane.
Sara likes to ride on a roller coaster.
Sara likes to ride a horse.
Sara likes to ride a bike.

There is no plot to this book, but if it is handmade, customized, or has high meaning, a plot will not matter (see samples of patterned books in appendixes). Customized books are adapted from books that have high meaning and appeal to individual reader interests and background (see Read-proofing a Book and Simplifying a Book).

One caveat critics cite is that readers are not really reading patterned books, but reciting them from memory (see Get 'em Reading First). This is a realistic possibility, especially for very young readers or those for whom the vocabulary is above independent reading level. There are several ways to correct memorizing the words, but I feel that memorization is a legitimate step in learning to read. If readers, especially poor ones, feel successful while memorizing, they have begun moving toward reading autonomy.

To encourage actual reading, immediately establish the following sequence:

1. Turn the page.
2. Look at the picture.
3. Read (with sweeping motion).

After every page is read, the tutor or teacher merely states, "Page—Picture—Read" (or uses some other signal, such as finger-snapping).

Reading, rather than simply having memorized, can be tested by pointing to an individual word in or out of sequence and asking readers to say the word. If students cannot, ask them to find the word in question by rereading the entire phrase in question, sweeping under the words as they read.

Prevention of memorization can also be done by read-proofing and administering the Middle-of-the-Book Test *before* allowing the student to read the book. If the words are too difficult, help him or her choose another patterned book (see Read-proofing a Book and Middle-of-the-Book Test).

Rationale

Predictable books are what they are called—predictable. Students do not have to struggle over what the words are, for the vocabulary is already familiar. These books build quick sight vocabularies, but the sight words are easily lost if not repeated in frequent rereading of the same story or by sightings in other books.

The "Page-Picture-Read" sequence ensures that:

1. Pictures give contextual clues that will help students read the text.

2. Students are not so likely to read part of a sentence and then look at the picture to help guess a particular word.

3. Sweeping, although not needed for every student, becomes an early habit for those who tend to lose their place or attention and need to focus on the words they are reading. When sweeping (focusing) is no longer needed, it drops off like a cocoon off a new butterfly, long before it is likely to slow down reading rate.

4. Sweeping makes learning more multimodal, involving motion and touch. The physical focus enhances the visual, mental, and oral focuses.

Phonics

Method

Although most readers are familiar with the term "phonics," they do not know how to teach it. A very thorough phonics program for busy experienced or inexperienced teachers to use in workbook form is published by Modern Curriculum Press (see chapter 4).

For the purposes of building fluency, this manual suggests using or teaching (at first) only a few phonics rules in the following order:

Consonant sounds such as /b/ (the slashes enclose the *sound,* "buh") as in ball.

Long vowel sounds: the sound of /a/ as in the letter "a." There are rules to teach the long vowel sounds:

1. If a word or syllable contains two vowels, the sound is *usually* long, as in *boat* and *came.*

2. The first vowel "speaks" while the other "listens." Some teachers say the first vowel does the talking while the other does the walking. In the word "boat," the /o/ is pronounced long /o/ as in letter "o," while /a/ is silent. In the word "came," the /a/ is pronounced long /a/ as in letter "a," while the /e/ is silent.

3. If a very short word or syllable ends in a vowel, it is *often* long (as in *me, be*fore).

Short vowel sounds: If a word or syllable contains one vowel followed by one or more consonants, it is *often* short (h*a*t, j*u*mp).

The short vowels can be taught by posting within easy view one-syllable sight words or objects that contain the sound of the short vowel. Examples are:

short /a/ as in cat
short /e/ as in red
short /i/ as in ship
short /o/ as in pop
short /u/ as in up

After students learn consonants and a long or short vowel sound, they need to learn how to blend the separate sounds into words. To teach the word "hand," for instance, ask, "What vowel sound is in this word?" When students choose the vowel sound, continue, "Begin the /h/, but don't let the sound come out until you are ready to make the short vowel sound /a/ like in *cat*." Guide them to pronounce /ha/. Continue, "Now close off /ha/ with a /t/." Have them drag the sound /ha/ until they stop it with the /t/.

I prefer to concentrate on the consonants, which are much more regular than the vowels, but I included the most simple vowel rules for those who would rather teach some vowel sounds prior to reading. For a more complete discussion on phonics, see chapter 1.

The following phonics rules can be added as or after the reader is reading fluently at his or her independent level—by the end of first grade or later.

Silent *e*
Hard and soft *c* and *g*
x sounds
Consonant clusters (2–3 letters, 2–3 sounds, as in *bl*ue)
Consonant digraphs (2 letters, 1 sound, as in *ph, gh, sh, ch, ng, wh, th).*
long *oo* (food)
short *oo* (look)
ew as in few
au and *aw* as in saw
ou and *ow* as in house
gu as in guard
r controlled vowels *(er, ar, or, ir, ur)*
syllables
simple prefixes and suffixes *(in, be, ing, s, d, ed)*

Many of the above rules can be pointed out to the reader in context as needed and repeated as often as necessary, regardless of what level the student is reading at. An example of teaching a phonics rule in context follows.

As a teacher reads a big book to a class of primary-age children, he or she may point to the letter "m" wherever it occurs on a certain page as follows: "Notice the 'm' in the word 'mouse.' Does it occur at the beginning, middle, or end of the word? How about in the word 'hummed?' 'ham?'"

The rest of the phonics rules tend to follow more regular Greek and Latin affixes; i.e., *"-ion, -ious, -ation"*, and can be taught in the third or fourth grades when vocabulary becomes more difficult.

Rationale

A more complete rationale is given in chapter 1, but much of it is from my own experience. I feel there is nothing wrong with following a complete graded phonics program, such as that developed by Modern Curriculum Press; however, many children cannot remember myriads of phonics rules. It is much easier to memorize the word. When you read a word, do you decode it? You probably recognize it instantly—you have memorized it. I feel phonics teaching will be less cumbersome and more meaningful if a substantial sight vocabulary can be referenced. Again, lest I be misunderstood for being "against" phonics, I teach a limited amount of phonics rules to begin with (consonants and possibly long and/or short vowels), followed by more advanced rules in the later levels.

Prompts and Cues

Method

Prompts and cues help the reader with word recognition, such as the size of the word, the only long word in the story, the word that fits the picture, the word printed in red or bold, the word that was discussed before the story was read, the word that always comes after another word, or the underlined word.

Rationale

These hints help beginning readers make educated or sensible word guesses, as opposed to wild ones, which occur from being introduced to too many words too quickly without prompts or cues. Some critics feel readers may depend too much on cues. It is my thesis that if a reader recognizes the word frequently within a short time frame, he or she will soon not need the prompt any longer.

Reader's Theater

See Scripted Reading.

Read-proofing a Book

Method

There are several ways to read-proof a book. First, categorize it (see Categorizing Books). Second, number its pages. Write the most difficult words and corresponding page numbers on a card, and put this card in a library card pocket mounted on the inside front cover. On side one of an audio cassette, clearly read each new word at a conversational pace, adding definitions if needed. If the book is difficult to understand, explain any unclear facts about setting, characters, plot, or objects. Include a question to set expectations and anticipation. However, do not preread the book to death or keep the child from getting started by "teacherizing" the book.

Explain the "Turn-the-page/Look-at-the-picture/Read" sequence (with the sweeping motion) on side B, if the tape is short and very easy to rewind, or on side A after the vocabulary words. The "turn-the-page" signal might be a bell, snapping fingers, clapping, strumming a guitar chord, or simply saying, "Turn the page." The sweeping motion requires the reader to move his or her fingers in a smooth motion underlining the words as they are read by the narrator at a regular conversational pace. Ask the reader to read the words while you read the book, using the sweeping motion. At the end of each page, your instructions can be shortened to "Page—Picture—Read."

If the book is technical, you may tell the reader not to expect to be able to whiz through it like a storybook but to anticipate learning valuable information. Expect that some paragraphs need to be read more than once. Talk about switching between pictures, diagrams, and text. Help the reader, especially in getting sequences and relationships straight, understanding cause-effect relationships, and relating parts to the overall picture. Tell why this book is worth reading, though not easy for everyone. Refer to specific pages where there may be obstacles to reading.

Rationale

The purpose for read-proofing a book is the same as

kid-proofing a house—protection from danger, protecting the reader, in this case, from attempting to read text that is too difficult, which can result in acquiring bad reading habits such as substituting or deleting words from the text. The principle is to give readers only the reading materials that they can read well enough to understand and enjoy.

The "Page-Picture-Read" sequence ensures that:

1. Pictures give contextual clues that will help students read the text.

2. Students are not likely to read part of a sentence and then look over to the picture to help guess a particular word.

3. Sweeping, although not needed for every student, becomes an early habit for those who tend to lose their place or attention and need to focus on the words they are reading. When sweeping (focusing) is no longer needed, students usually stop.

4. Sweeping makes learning more multimodal, involving motion and touch. The physical focus enhances the visual, mental, and oral focuses.

Rereading

Method

The student reads a selection he or she has already read, immediately or the next day after having read the material the first time. Students can reread any number of times, depending on fluency. The following are a few suggested variations for rereading:

> Read silently while teacher or a tape recording reads aloud.
>
> Read aloud for expression.
>
> Read as quickly as possible to build speed. Decode, ask, or find unrecognized words *after* rereading is finished.
>
> Read the same passage to different people (classmates, relatives, neighbors, etc.).

Rereading works best when combined with the Middle-of-the-Book Test. The student says, "I'm done with this story." The teacher administers the Middle-of-the-Book Test and sends the student back for another rereading if fluency is not yet achieved. After several tries, students need only to reread a certain page that contains key words missed.

The number of rereadings varies with student need and purpose; sometimes students need only to reread a certain page or paragraph that contains key words missed. At first, beginners may need to reread many times, especially when continually reading new vocabulary. If using basal readers, rereadings can be less because new words are sequenced and repeated. A beginner's first story of two words might be read five times; if ten-fifteen words, perhaps six or seven. As a core vocabulary is built, students need fewer rereadings. Slower learners always need to reread more than brighter students. Adults need rereading as much as children. As stories increase in length, five times might be an average; some students might get by with less.

If students reread more than three times with no improvement, however, teachers need to check the difficulty of the book or student reading habits. Many students, especially the very bright, add or delete words from the text in a sloppy effort to "get ahead." Sometimes they get into such bad habits they cannot be trusted to read or reread alone and must do so aloud with a trained reader (see Alternate Reading Exercise, ARE Cloze, Paired and Parroted Reading, and Whole Passage method, which are all forms that can be used for rereading).

Rationale

This is the simplest and most effective of fluency-building methods, providing easy practice on the same material for the student. It is often combined with other methods, such as Whole Passage, Phonics, Comprehension, and Vocabulary Drill. The number of times Rereading occurs depends on the fluency the student or teacher desires to achieve.

Some teachers, upon first hearing of the regular use of Rereading, respond, How would you get kids to do that? Why would they want to reread a story when they already know the ending?

I wish all such teachers could visit a classroom where Rereading is routinely working very well. The children do not question it, providing they know they will not have to reread a story if it is mastered and they find the stories are worth rereading.

It is important for the reader to repeat the selection close enough to the original reading to reinforce the new words being learned to the point of automaticity. If a selection is read once and the words are not sighted again for several weeks, students will likely not recognize them without prompts or cues.

When a student rereads a selection, he or she will gain

meanings formerly misunderstood or missed in the first reading, improving comprehension. Rereading ensures honesty and mastery; i.e., students do not fudge or cheat on their reading when they know they will have to do it over again anyway if it is not right.

Scripted Reading

Method

The teacher finds (or writes) a selection which includes direct quotes by different characters. The selection can be any story on the independent or instructional levels, such as one from a basal reader or favorite library book. The teacher makes one copy per student, highlighting the part of one character in each copy. To have enough parts, teachers can divide narration into "Narrator #1," "Narrator #2," etc. He or she can also assign onomatopoeic parts, such as "fire truck," "water," "ducks," or "car" ("Honk, honk!"). Each part is labeled, highlighted, and given out ahead of time for practice.

Rationale

Scripted reading is a way to encourage oral reading while eliminating the negative aspects of embarrassing poor readers and boring good ones. Reading parts captures the interest and imagination of students who like play-acting and pretending and provides a safe, nonthreatening forum for shy students. Practicing ahead ensures success, especially if teacher- or parent-supervised.

Simplifying a Book

Method

This method can be used for the student's personal library or the classroom library. The following adaptation is for classroom use.

1. Purchase several copies of a reasonably-priced book, if possible, enough that each student or pair of students can read the book. Look for books with similar pictures of the same group, such as pictures of different animals or activities.

2. Depending on the reading level needed, type or write in new words that can be pasted over the old text or use rubber cement to cut and paste large-sized print over the old text. If possible, use a pattern, such as "I took a picture of a ___" with each animal or object.

3. Pass the books out in class and teach the "Turn-the-page/Look-at-the-picture/Read" sequence (with sweeping motion), as in Patterned or Predictable Book Reading. You can also use Read-proofing a Book or Whole Passage method with these books.

A variation might be to purchase a book of a favorite story or movie, such as Walt Disney's *Pocahontas* or James Herron's dog stories, and rewrite the text in simplified language. In books like James Herron's, one can purchase two paperback copies, cutting out and using both sides of the pages. Pictures and text can be cut and pasted so that simplified text is on the top half of the page, and the original text is on the bottom half. These cut-up and pasted pages can be mounted on 8 1/2 x 11 paper and inserted into clear plastic sheet protectors in a notebook. Later, when students achieve advanced reading levels, they can read the original text.

Rationale

Often teachers "inherit" books in their classrooms which are not suitable to the reading levels of the class. If funds and book inventory are low, this is a way to redeem rather than give away books which have potential for beginning readers. Sometimes a teacher, parent, or tutor may wish to "downsize" reading levels for a favorite story, classic, or book with beautiful pictures, but yet preserve the higher level text.

"Speed" Reading

Method

This is not really speed reading, but several helpful methods to speed up students' reading.

1. If students read silently more slowly than they speak, have them read orally for speed in a private location. They can alternately read for accuracy, then for speed. Words that are persistently missed can be repeated five times in a row right after they are missed.

2. While the leader reads the selection aloud at a fast pace, students can practice reading material line by line

instead of word by word. Later they can practice reading sentence by sentence and ultimately, paragraph by paragraph (providing paragraphs are short and sentences are simple).

Rationale

Students experience success when they have control and can vary their own speeds. Practice of familiar material is the best way to build fluency, for reading, like typing and piano playing, can be practiced at ever-increasing speeds.

Student's Unassisted Reading Exercise (SURE)

See Oral Reading.

Sustained Silent Reading (SSR)

Method

In some schools, this method is called DEAR (Drop Everything And Read). Students silently read at their independent levels in their interest areas in a quiet classroom for a sustained period (anywhere from ten minutes for early first graders to thirty minutes for more mature students). Interest levels of books should be high. Students can read books of their own choice at their level and/or reread selections they have recently learned (see Categorizing Books).

Rationale

It is crucial that students read at their independent level in order for this method to work. It has been my experience that when given a choice, most students choose books that are too difficult for them—largely because there is not a diverse enough selection at their level to hold their interest. (For a complete explanation and how-tos, see Myers and Oliphant 1994, and Fielding and Roller 1992. Also, see Tapping for Words in this chapter).

By reading at their independent levels, students are reinforcing vocabulary they already know and practicing good reading habits. To ensure successful SSR, enough time must be made available for students not to be frustrated with interruptions or insufficient time to finish a selection long enough to hold their interest. Some teachers try to use silent reading to "fill in" gaps of two minutes until recess, or five minutes until the other group finishes. Such discontinuous reading is so uninteresting and frustrating that it can contribute to dislike of reading.

Tapping for Words

Method

During sustained, silent reading, leaders can tell readers, "If you see a word you need help with, just tap lightly on your desk. I'll say the word right away." The leader is ready to offer assistance as needed, in a pleasant tone. Teaching how to decode a word can be done later.

Rationale

Students can continue reading while getting help without looking up from the text. This method relieves students from having to engage in any laborious decoding that would interrupt comprehension and flow of thought. However, teachers often read their own material during Sustained Silent Reading, which results in students not getting timely help, thus encouraging loss of concentration and distraction. (See also Tell the Word.)

Teacher-Orchestrated
Oral Reading Exercise (TOORE)

See Oral Reading.

Tell the Word

Method

When a student gets stuck on a word, tell the word without requiring that he or she try to decode it. A teacher, parent, or peer can function as word teller.

Variations include signals students use for help, as in Tapping for Words—tapping a pencil or other object three times on the desk; raising hands; putting up a place card on the desk which signifies "help needed"; asking a neighbor or designated peer leader-for-the-day.

Rationale

This method is best used during sustained silent reading

time. Students get annoyed when their reading is interrupted by having to decode ("sound out") or look up an unknown word in the dictionary, often skipping the word to go on without interruption, and comprehension may or may not be sacrificed. To avoid comprehension problems and establish the habit of mastering unknown words, teachers simply tell the child the word. Decoding and other word attack methods may be taught at other times.

Unison

Method

Students read every page or paragraph, or alternate pages or paragraphs, with a leader simultaneously. Variations include: alternating Unison reading with Cloze (students chime in at designated places); reading preprimers or whole stories in unison; and singing song lyrics (reading them by singing in unison).

Rationale

Used in combination with the whole passage method, Unison reading is another form of practice or drill, while enabling the instructor to monitor reading proficiency.

Vocabulary Drill

Method

There are many versions of vocabulary or word drill,

and they are usually done before or after reading. Word drill can be done on lists of single words, phrases of two words, phrases of three words, or short sentences. When the word list includes both single words and two-word phrases, list the single words first. When word drill includes phrases of two or three words, list the two-word phrases first. Teacher or student may point to the words. Try these variations and make your own:

1. Read new words to students first.

2. Show differences between new words and words which look alike (invincible, invisible).

3. First drill slowly, then speed up the pace.

4. Repeat each word or phrase twice together (invincible, invincible).

5. Repeat each word or phrase with the teacher.

6. Use an established routine (advantages: no directions, no talking, lack of resistance; force of habit takes over).

7. Point out noticeable phonetic features (this starts with "m"; the "ph" sounds like "f").

8. Teach them to "sweep" words or lines with fingers and/or eyes.

9. If one student in a group gets lost as you proceed down the list, tell him or her to join in when he or she can.

10. Warn students to expect to make mistakes aloud, and that it is "ok".

11. Say the words sometimes in rhythm, sometimes not.

12. Say the word sometimes silently, sometimes out loud.

13. Say the word sometimes in unison, sometimes individually.

14. Follow each word with one or two claps, snaps, pointing, or jumping, in rhythm: "Satisfied, satisfied" (clap); "Tomorrow, tomorrow" (clap).

15. Ask a student to point to the word as he or she repeats it.

Rationale

Word drill can be made fun with creative variations. It serves to enhance word recognition and repeat sightings until the word is recognized instantly and effortlessly. Some students will benefit more than others from this method, and you may want to adapt it to visual, auditory, and tactile learners (those who learn by touching and feeling objects).

Whole Passage

Method

This is a way to teach an entire reading selection at the

instructional level. The selection is usually short, and presenting it on one page on the overhead projector makes it possible to use the strategy with a large group. After the teacher/tutor does the initial reading, and the students have read along silently, use creative methods to reread the selection.

There are many different ways to read a whole passage, but the main idea of each variation is for the student or teacher to read the *entire* selection or portion of a selection at once. Variations include:

1. Teacher or parent reads the selection while student(s) listen.

2. Teacher or parent reads passage while student(s) read along silently.

3. Teacher or parent asks certain student(s) to read parts or all of the selection with him or her (i.e., those with blue eyes or wearing jeans first, followed by those who do *not* have blue eyes or are not wearing jeans).

4. Passage can be projected from a transparency to a screen, written on the board or large newsprint, printed on a handout, a big book, or in a textbook.

5. Passage can be read in unison.

6. Teacher can use other methods on the passage (i.e., Alternate Reading Exercise, Cloze, Parroted Reading, and Paired Reading).

For other variations of the Whole Passage method, see the Language Experience and Unison methods.

Rationale

The whole passage method gets readers to reread and thus practice material as many times as possible. It differs from sight methods that teach words in isolation in that words are learned in context. Perhaps the main goal of whole passage reading is to build high and quick comprehension by having students hear or read the entire selection in one sitting.

Research on the whole passage method supports holistic, integrated learning with studies that show increased fluency and vocabulary development. The whole passage method has been shown to be one of the most efficient ways to build vocabulary. Because it offers context clues and high comprehension, students can learn more new words more quickly than if learning them in isolation. For this reason, adults learn well when they are read to first from a book that may be above their instructional level, but which has high personal meaning. If the second reading is in unison, they often can read a whole chapter the third time with medium support (such as Alternate Reading Exercise or Paired Reading).

Word Attack

Method

When a reader encounters an unfamiliar word, he or she can use all or a portion of the following methods to decode the word:

1. Read to the end of the sentence (for contextual clues).

2. Look at the picture and reread.

3. Ask, *"Does it look right?"* (initial letter sound; more mature readers also check vowel, middle, and ending sounds).

4. Ask, *"Does it make sense?"* (for contextual meaning).

5. Ask, *"Does it sound right?"* (for grammar and usage—would we say it that way?).

6. Read on and/or ask for help.

Rationale

When students encounter a new word, they need to have some strategies that will help them learn it. Most students genuinely wonder what the word is, and, if they had some tools, would try decoding. If they are successful, vocabulary is improved and so is their self-confidence.

Word Drill

See Vocabulary Drill.

Wordless Books

Method

Wordless books are children's books with pictures that tell a story but have no text. They are available from major publishers of children's books and libraries.

These books are helpful for teaching young emergent readers how to read from left to right, how to learn the parts of a book, including the title page, how to turn pages, and how to read pictures. They can also be used as a variation of the Language Experience method, in which a child can dictate a story, using simple language, to describe the pictures in a wordless book. The teacher/tutor can then use the Instant Sight Reading method or Whole Passage method to teach the story the child made.

Rationale

Wordless books play a part in emergent reading, helping young children learn "how books work." The method is particularly useful for emergent readers and students who have not been read to at home.

4

Resources for Beginning Readers

Although there is a great need for it, book publishers, vendors, and libraries usually do not organize books for the needs of beginning readers. This condition may be changing, but on a very limited scale. If you walk into a bookstore, library, or school library, or even if you look at a publisher's catalog of juvenile books or books for reading teachers to order for their classrooms, you will likely not find books for beginning readers categorized according to levels. This chapter exists for this reason—to help you discover what materials are available at various levels.

For adults and adolescents, the problem is much worse! Low-level readers with mature interest levels are so specialized that they are not readily available, even in many junior colleges that teach remedial reading classes. Therefore, I have listed the kinds of places where one is apt to find these select resources.

Since publishers do not, for the most part, perform the service of grading the reading levels of books for beginning readers, and since there is no standardized English system for finding the reading levels of English books, reading teachers and parents may try using *readability estimators.* These handy guides, listed under computer software in this chapter or in the appendix (Fry's Readability Graph), help analyze the average grade level of a book. They are not foolproof—it is usually safer to use more than one formula and to listen to students read selections before assigning a level to a book—but reading formulas can give one a fair idea of the vocabulary or grade level of a book. As mentioned in chapter 3, however, the teacher can find out if a book is at an appropriate level by simply listening to the student read (see Categorizing Books and Middle-of-the-Book Test in chapter 3).

One must remember, however, that many readability estimators, including Fry's, have limitations—they grade only on the basis of sentence length, number of syllables per word, and the like. While these are key factors, other components not measured by such formulas—such as familiarity with subject matter and illustrations, word or sentence repetition (patterning), amount and helpfulness of illustrations, and extent of unusual, specialized vocabulary and literary language—also affect readability (Peterson, B. n.d.). These factors vary with individuals, which is why reading is so highly individualized and should be taught in a similar manner.

In addition to readability estimators, books, and catalogs, several other resources are listed, including software, newspapers, magazines, workbooks, articles, and books for adolescent, adult, and young readers.

Resources for Adult Beginning Readers

Older beginning readers, especially teenagers, tend to recoil at having to read books with young children's graphics. There are a variety of resources available at low reading levels with high interest levels and mature graphics for adult reading. These resources, which include textbooks and workbooks in GED (High School Grade Equivalency Diploma) subject areas, paperback novels, magazines, and newspapers, are often available through adult learning centers at local high schools or ESL (English as a Second Language) centers. A sampling of publishers who publish catalogues or newspapers that include this level of resources is listed below, but some of the sources listed under Resources for Children and Software are also appropriate for teens and adults, especially some of the inexpensive word processing programs.

Curriculum Associates
5 Esquire Road
North Billerica, MA 01862-2589
1-800-225-0248 or 505-667-8000
FAX 508-667-5706

Send for their *Adult-Vocational-Secondary Catalog.*

Globe Fearon Educational Publisher
4350 Equity Drive
POB 2649
Columbus, OH 43216
1-800-848-9500
FAX 614-771-7361

This publisher publishes low-level books for adult readers

on many subjects, including GED preparation. Examples include some paperback readers, eighty pages each, with a grade 3.5 reading level and a grade 6–12 interest level. Prices range from $5.70 for single copies to $4.20 each when purchased in sets of ten different books. Some sets include skill tests for each reader. These readers are good for practice in building fluency. Phonics and word attack skills are available in various reading program workbooks that may or may not accompany the readers. One of the reader-workbook sets costs $12. A spelling program is also available.

News for You
New Readers Press
Department 26
Box 131
Syracuse, NY 13210-9988
1-800-448-8878, M–F 8–8 EST

News For You is a newspaper of world events, political issues, and business news written for adolescent and adult learners on levels 4–6. It also offers a wide variety of other news, including health, sports, people, and a crossword puzzle.

New Readers Press
Department 26
Box 131
Syracuse, NY 13210
1-800-448-8878, M–F 8–8 EST

New Readers Press offers over 300 publications for ESL and Adult Ed students and readers of all levels and ages.

Steck-Vaughn Company
POB 2028
Austin, TX 76788

This publisher offers a variety of phonics, comprehension, reading, and writing activities for adolescent and adult learners. Some books offer themes which are carefully chosen to reflect the interest of today's adolescent reader: favorite TV or sports stars, etc.

Resources for Children

Books for Young Readers

Bob Books
Box 633
West Linn, OR 97068
503-657-1883

Bob books are three sets ($15 per set) of eight tiny booklets for young, grade one, first-time readers, available in children's educational stores. Each level becomes incrementally more difficult. It is hard to find interesting readers with lively scenarios or plots that begin with just one word on a page, but these readers fit the bill.

Benefic Press

Benefic no longer publishes, but they did publish low-level reading books of good character, high morals, and high interest for children. If you can find them in libraries or garage sales, books by Benefic Press are excellent.

Bradshaw Publishers
POB 277
Bryn Mawr, CA 92318

Publishes *Bible Stories for Early Readers,* appropriate for young children and available in Christian bookstores.

Follett Publishers
5563 S. Archer Ave.
Chicago, IL 60638
1-800-621-4272

Follett collects and distributes used textbooks and workbooks used in public and private schools.

Library & Educational Services
8784 Valley View Drive
Berrien Springs, MI 49103
1-616-471-1400

A good discount dealer for educational institutions, libraries, home schools, and parents. They handle Christian and other educational materials for all ages.

Modern Curriculum Press
13900 Prospect Road
Cleveland, OH 44136

Besides publishing a good phonics series, this press offers excellent beginning reading books in Spanish and English.

Murr's Library Book Service
4045 E. Palm Lane, Suite #5
Phoenix AZ 85008

602-273-1121

A good discount dealer for children's educational books.

Questar Publishers, Inc.
POB 1720
Sisters, OR 97759

Publishes the *Early Reader's Bible* ($10) available in Christian bookstores.

Random House Books and More Back List Catalog
Random House Juvenile Division
201 E. 50th St.
New York, NY 10022
212-940-7695

Readers must examine such book catalogs with care. For example, if one were to look at this catalog, he or she would have to hunt under the following headings to find juvenile beginning readers: First-time Readers, Bright and Early Books, Beginner Books, Step Into Reading (only Step One and Step Two), Random House Picture Backs, and Sesame Street Start-to-Read Books. None of these readers can be found in one list, and they may not all be graded according to reading levels.

Patterned (Predictable) Books

Most patterned books are written for children (see chapter 3, Patterned or Predictable Book Reading). Two sample patterned books are included in the appendixes. Patterning is everywhere, especially in songs ("The wheels on the bus go 'round and 'round...") and poetry. Good patterning sources are Modern Curriculum Press (see address below under Phonics Workbook), the *Early Reader's Bible,* ($10, Questar Publishers, Inc., POB 1720, Sisters, OR 97759), appropriate for young children; and the Dr. Seuss books (Beginner Books, 201 E. 50th St., New York, NY 10022, 212-751-2600) available in most bookstores and libraries. The Wright Group, 19201 120th Ave. NE, Bothell, WA 98011-9512, 1-800-523-2371, FAX 206-486-7868, publishes *Sunshine Books* and other predictable books. A good selection of patterned books for children is available from publishers and most bookstores. The best way to find them is to browse in libraries and bookstores.

Periodicals

Some of the following magazines, although written for children, are appropriate for adults and adolescents. If you have never heard of these periodicals, most publishers will send a sample copy; some will allow a trial subscription for a couple of weeks or months. Many are also available through public or private school and community libraries. Some publishers know the reading or interest level of their periodicals; if not, you can use Fry's Readability Graph to determine the level yourself. Many of these periodicals have teacher's helps and activities for children that work well with the Activity-Based Reading method in chapter 3.

3-2-1 Contact
POB 53051
Boulder, CO 80322-3051

A science magazine for the middle grades following the PBS–TV format.

Cobblestone
30 Grove St.
Peterborough, NH 03458

Offers *Cobblestone,* a history magazine for grades 4–9, and *Faces,* magazine biographies also for grades 4–9.

God's World
Box 2330
Asheville, NC 28802-2330
1-800-951-5437

Offers Christian world newspapers at six different reading levels from pre–K through adult, including one for pre–K, one for grade 1, and one for grades 2–3. Prices range from $18–19.50/year to $5/year for one newspaper, depending on the number of subscriptions you order. A variety of educational activities for teachers and students accompany the newspapers, and the news covered is a variety of political and human interest issues of educational value.

National Geographic World
POB 2330
Washington, D. C. 20077

Colorful photography with simplified text modeled after the adult version, for grades 3–6.

Ranger Rick Magazine
National Wildlife Federation
8925 Leesburg Pike
Vienna, VA 22184-0001

A nature magazine with interesting activities, often

including wildlife posters, for grades 3–6.

Scholastic, Inc.
POB 3410
Jefferson City, MO 65102-3710

Offers many pertinent publications:

> *Scholastic Math Power,* grades 1–3
> *Scholastic DynaMath,* grades 4–6
> *Scholastic News,* Social Studies weekly for grades 1–6
> *Super Science Blue,* grades 4–8. $11.50
> *Super Science Red,* grades K–3. $11.50

Science Weekly, Inc.
2141 Industrial Parkway, Suite 202
Silver Spring, MD 20904
301-680-8804

Levels A–E for Pre–K to grade 6. $8.95 ($4 for over 20 subscriptions).

Weekly Reader.
Field Publications
4343 Equity Drive
Columbus, OH 43216

Weekly news for grades 1–6 available in English or Spanish.

Phonics Workbook

Modern Curriculum Press
13900 Prospect Road
Cleveland, OH 44136

Issues a graded phonics series, the "MCP Phonics Program," that is thorough and easy to understand.

Software

The following is a sampling of reading software available for your PC. Unless noted, all programs can be ordered from:

Educational Resources
1550 Executive Drive
Elgin, IL 60123
1-800-624-2926 (outside IL)
1-708-888-8300 (in IL)
1-708-888-8499/8689 (FAX)

Most programs are in the $30–70 range (at time of publishing) if purchased from large educational software distributors such as Educational Resources, listed above, and, unless specified, are available for MAC, Apple, and IBM computers. Most include CD Rom or Windows versions. Many programs will "talk" if your computers have speech synthesizer software installed.

There are many reviews of reading and language arts software programs in the literature, and some are listed in the bibliography. Gunning's and Dublin's books, listed under References, are good resources.

The Accelerated Reader. $300. This program can be purchased only from Advantage Learning System, Inc., 2610 Industrial Street, POB 36, Wisconsin Rapids, WI 54495-0036, 715-424-3636 or 1-800-338-4204. FAX 715-424-4242. It includes hundreds of tests to supplement or accompany school or public library books. The program classifies the hundreds of literature books it tests according to Fry's Readability Graph (not foolproof, but better than none). Therefore, teachers and librarians have an instant reference guide to the reading level of the library books their students choose or need. The tests, ranging from 5–20 questions, depending on which level, come on floppy disks of 200 tests for $300 for each level from K–high school. Teachers can use these tests to monitor whether students are reading the books they check out. A computer point system rewards reading, and the computer record-keeping system monitors individual reading in large classes.

Bailey's Book House. $36-43. Teaches beginning reading skills to children.

Big Book Maker. $50 each title. Makes books from 8 1/2" x 11" to 37 feet tall. Ten different programs allow students to write their own big books with predetermined sets.

CORE Reading and Vocabulary Development Program. $79–159. Available from Educational Activities, Inc., POB 392, Freeport, NY 11520. 1-800-645-3739; in New York, 516-223-4666. This publisher offers the CORE reading and vocabulary development program in English and Spanish with adult interest level and reading levels as low as pre-primer. It is designed for students whose primary language is other than English.

Creative Writer. $28. This delightful writing and desktop publishing program takes children through revolving doors into Imagineland, etc., to create illustrated stories, newsletters, banners, and greeting cards.

Dr. Peet's Talk/Writer. $39. Any age beginning reader. Teaches letter recognition, keyboarding, and word processing (combining letters to form words). The program "speaks" to students by pronouncing letters.

Imagination Express Series. $23 each title (6 titles), CD only. Children create books on beautiful backgrounds.

Intensive Phonics Program. $800 complete. Curriculum Associates, Inc., 5 Esquire Road, North Billerica, MA 01862-2589. 1-800-225-0248. Three levels for grades 1–8 or ESL students (adult graphics may be ready at the time this manual is published). The levels are not sold separately, but there are volume discounts.

Just Grandma and Me. $38 CD Rom only. This story with colorful graphics is read to children in English, Spanish, or Japanese.

Kid Phonics. $39 CD only. Teaches children letter sounds and words.

Kid Works II, Kid Works Deluxe, Kid Works Bilingual. $36–100. For primary grades. With this word processor, children can paint and write their own stories or rebus stories in large, primary font on primary lines. Stories are read back to them (if your computer has speaker capabilities). *Kid Works II* is the floppy version, and *Kid Works Deluxe,* the CD Rom, which is easier to use and offers more options. *Kid Works Bilingual* ($100) offers a Spanish/English version.

Language Experience Recorder. $84. For primary grades. This program offers a choice of fonts and prints out vocabulary randomly, alphabetically, or according to frequency. It makes large charts for whole class reading or small pages. A readability index reads stories you write, automatically indexing their grade level.

Make-a-Book. $40. This program prints your story in fonts and booklets of various sizes with a title page. Excellent for making patterned books.

National Geographic Kid's Network. $300. For primary and middle grades. Available from National Geographic Kid's Network, Educational Services, Box 98018, Washington, DC 20090, 1-800-368-2728. Although used mostly in schools, anyone who has access to on-line materials through a computer modem can access this network for a fee. Children's programs run throughout the school year, connecting students working on science projects to other pupils all over the world. Students collect and compare data and read suggested materials.

Once Upon a Time, Vols. 1–4. $40 per volume or $80 per set. This delightful story maker for primary grades has many different backdrops—the child chooses a picture and types a few lines of text below. The story makes a beautifully-illustrated booklet or page on a color printer.

Picture Phonics. $42. Phonics activities for young children.

Readability Analysis. $35.95 IBM only. Type in a passage from a book, and this program will use one of its readability formulas to grade the reading level of the text for you. There are three different formulas to choose from: Spache Primary Reading Formula, grades 1–3; Dale Chall Formula, grades 4–college; and the Fry Readability

Formula, grades 1–college. The Fry is usually used as a second reference for the other two formulas.

Readability Program. $44.95 Apple; $49.95 MAC, DOS, Windows. Micro Power & Light Co., 8814 Sanshire Ave., Dallas, TX 75231. 214-553-0105. This program automatically determines K–12 readability levels of text according to several different formulas, depending on the version, including Dale Chall, Fry, Flesch, Fog, and Spache.

Reader Rabbit's Interactive Reading Journey. $86–110. This program offers 40 progressively-challenging books for young children with "read-to-me" or "read-it-myself" options and skills components.

Stickybear's Early Learning Activities. $36. Teaches alphabet and other early concepts in English and Spanish.

Stickybear Reading. $28. Besides learning many reading skills, children create sentences illustrated by animations.

Stickybear's Reading Room. $37. This bilingual English and Spanish program teaches prereading and reading skills.

Storybook Maker Deluxe. $22 CD only. Children or tutors can record and play their own stories using a variety of backgrounds.

Storybook Weaver Deluxe. $47 CD only. Students can choose from mythical character graphics to create their own stories.

Urban Reader. $185. This multilingual collection of 48 stories are for grades 6–adult, with reading levels 4–9.

The Vocabulary Assessor. $89.95. Micro Power & Light Co., 8814 Sanshire Ave., Dallas, TX 75231. 214-553-0105. This program compares reading selections on your word processor's document text files to a second file consisting of your student's vocabulary, listing difficult words alphabetically or in order of frequency. Typical grade-level vocabulary lists are available for $35 per level.

Write Now. $43 MAC only. A good word processing program with graphics, dictionary, thesaurus, and grammar checker for older children to adults.

The Writing Center, The Bilingual Writing Center, Student Writing Center, Children's Writing and Publishing Center, The Ultimate Writing and Creativity Center. $73–$166. These powerful word processing programs are for Grades 2 and up. Students can design and produce illustrated reports, newsletters, signs, cards, calendars, and more. Depending on the version, they include spell checker, thesaurus, and graphics and can print in color. *Writing Center* and *Bilingual Writing Center* (English and Spanish) are only available on MAC, while *Student Writing Center* is the Windows version. *Children's Writing and Publishing Center* is an older program offering fewer options, but still an excellent word processing program. *The Ultimate Writing and Creativity Center* adds clip art, sound, and animation to colorful backgrounds for multimedia presentations.

Young Authors. $54–150. This bilingual program creates up to 25 different types of books (pop-ups, shape books, reports, joke book, and more) in English and Spanish.

Appendix A

Dolch Basic Sight Words

The basic vocabulary of Dolch "service words" includes many "function words" that have little meaning by themselves, such as "a," "the," and "and." You can give these words more meaning by teaching them in a personalized sentence context.

In the following sentences, all 220 Dolch Basic Words are used at least once. Type these sentences on a large-print typewriter or computer. Leave blanks to fill in the words the reader supplies. Of course, do only a few at a time and use only after you have used the Instant Sight Reading method (see chapter 3) for beginning vocabulary. Each child or adult can use or have his or her own personalized set of cards. Students can drill themselves on these words and rearrange them for greater meaning. You will see that more words than 220 are learned on these pages, but many may have already been learned with the Instant Sight

Reading method, and the rest are easily learned because of strong context clues and personal meaning.

I said, "I must call _____."
_____went to _____ with _____.
I know where to find _____.
I have one _____ and two _____ and three _____ and
　　four _____ and five _____ and six _____ and
　　seven _____ and eight____ and nine _____ and
　　ten _____ which are my own.
I will always _____.
I will never _____.
I will sometimes _____.
I thank _____ for _____.
I drink _____ down fast.
I can cut _____.
I would like to _____ because _____.
I had to buy a long _____.
Yes, I can jump off _____.
I wish I could _____.
Many people run around _____.
I wash my _____ until it is clean; then I stop washing.
I have been very _____.
My _____ was hurt, but now it's very much better.
My best _____ is yellow.
Tell me how to write a _____.
Ask _____ to sing something pretty.
Come again to see me after _____.
I am playing around _____.
As soon as I start _____, I would like to have the light
　　off.
I will be far away from _____.
It is best to work before _____.
A big _____ is better than a small one.

My blue _____ came from _____.

I would buy a black horse for _____.

I would buy a new brown house by _____ for _____.

Shall I call _____ tonight?

Could we eat a cold _____ together?

Do you sleep under a warm _____ every night?

I can draw a _____ by myself.

Once I did something funny that made _____ laugh.

Your dog does _____.

Don't _____ until you're done _____.

Draw _____ jumping into _____.

_____ may fall down _____ if _____.

The first time I fly in a _____, I am going to take _____ with me.

I found a _____ which came from _____.

I got a _____ full of _____.

_____ gave to _____ a little _____.

If I get much money, I will get a good _____ for _____.

I am going to give _____ something that will grow.

There goes a green _____.

He has to know how to read _____.

Help her use her _____.

Help him fix his _____.

Who will help us put the _____ up on the _____?

_____ and I were walking fast.

_____ went to the hospital to get well.

I want to eat _____ when I get home.

My _____ was white when it was new. (Or make plural form)

My _____ is sitting upon my _____.

These are my _____. Give them to me.

Tell them to take _____ to _____.

Shall I sit in front of _____ or shall I sit over here?

I saw something so small that if I show it to _____ he won't see it at all.

If you see a fire, open this and pull that, and then run right out this door. (No words to fill in)

Call the men who ride around in the red fire truck to come fast. (No words to fill in)

Only pick the right numbers to call. (No words to fill in)

I want to know why _____.

I know where _____.

When I grow up, I will not _____.

I know what to do if _____.

I like my old _____ better than my _____.

No, you should never _____.

Do not put something hot into this _____.

They need to keep their own _____ at _____.

This kind of plant can live in _____.

_____ looks just like _____.

Once I made a _____ by myself.

I can make _____, too.

I ran from our _____ to our _____.

I will try to do _____ well today.

I think those _____ are very pretty.

Appendix B

Fry's Instant Words: First Hundred[1]

These are the most common words in English, ranked in order of frequency, for beginning readers of any age. The first 25 make up about a third of all printed material, and the first 100, about half.

The first 100 words are followed by lists of the second and third 100 words, along with uses and applications, in *1000 Instant Words* (Fry 1994). These lists are useful for creating beginning reading books using core reading vocabularies (see Core Vocabulary in chapter 3).

---

[1]Courtesy of Edward Fry, Rutgers University.

Fry's Instant Words:
First Hundred

1–25	*26–50*	*51–75*	*76–100*
the	or	will	number
of	one	up	no
and	had	other	way
a	by	about	could
to	word	out	people
in	but	many	my
is	not	then	than
you	what	them	first
that	all	these	water
it	were	so	been
he	we	some	call
was	when	her	who
for	your	would	oil
on	can	make	now
are	said	like	find
as	there	him	long
with	use	into	down
his	an	time	day
they	each	has	did
I	which	look	get
at	she	two	come
be	do	more	made
this	how	write	may
have	their	go	part
from	if	see	over

Appendix C

Fry's Readability Graph[1]

Instructions

1. Randomly select three passages and count out exactly 100 words each, beginning with the beginning of a sentence. Do count proper nouns, initializations, and numerals.

2. Count the number of sentences in the hundred words, estimating length of the fraction of the last sentence to the nearest one-tenth.

3. Count the total number of syllables in the 100-word passage. If you do not have a hand counter available, simply put a mark above every syllable other than the

---

[1]Courtesy of Edward Fry, Rutgers University.

first syllable in each word. When you get to the end of the passage, count the number of marks and add 100. Small calculators can also be used as counters by pushing numeral 1 first, then pushing the + sign for each word or syllable.

4. Graph with *average* sentence length and *average* number of syllables; plot dot where the two lines intersect. Area where dot is plotted will give you the approximate grade level.

5. If a great deal of variability is found in syllable count or sentence count, putting more samples into the average is desirable.

6. A word is defined as a group of symbols with a space on either side; thus, "Joe," "IRA," "1945," and "&" are each one word.

7. A syllable is defined as a phonetic syllable. Generally, there are as many syllables as vowel sounds. For example, *stopped* is one syllable and *wanted* is two syllables. When counting syllables for numerals and initializations, count one syllable for each symbol. For example, 1945 is four syllables.

Example:

	Syllables	Sentences
1st Hundred Words	124	6.6
2nd Hundred Words	141	5.5
3rd Hundred Words	158	6.8
Averages	141	6.3

Readability 7th grade (see dot plotted on graph)

Fry's Readability Graph[1]

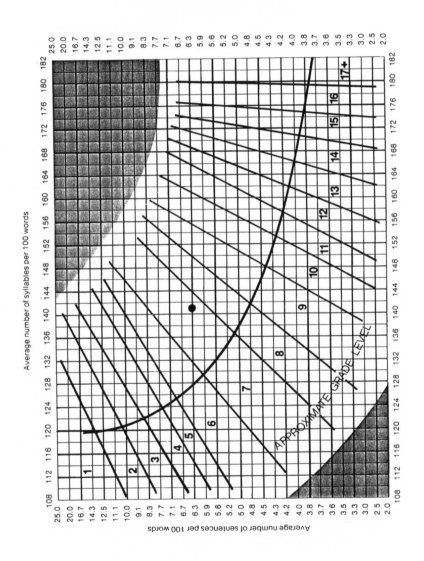

[1]Courtesy of Edward Fry, Rutgers University.

Appendix D

Sample of a Patterned Book:
The Bridge Is Out

This is only the text of an unpublished patterned, predictable story, which, incidentally, happened in a town in which I lived. Ideally, a full-page illustration should face each page of text. The vocabulary is not for an *early* beginning reader; for samples of how to plan patterned, predictable books for early readers, see chapter 3.

Page 1
The flood washed the bridge out.

Page 2
A policeman warned the tractor driver, "Go back! The bridge is out!"
"Okay," said the tractor driver, "I cannot fix the bridge."

Page 3

A policeman warned the fire truck driver, "Go back! The bridge is out!"

"Okay," said the fire truck driver, "I cannot fix the bridge."

Page 4

A policewoman warned the ice cream truck driver, "Go back! The bridge is out!"

"Okay," said the ice cream truck driver, "I cannot fix the bridge."

Page 5

A policewoman warned the cement truck driver, "Go back! The bridge is out!"

"Okay," said the cement truck driver. "I cannot fix the bridge *yet.*"

Page 6

A policewoman warned the motorcycle driver, "Go back! The bridge is out!"

"Okay," said the motorcycle driver, "I cannot fix the bridge."

Page 7

A policeman warned the tricycle driver, "Go back! The bridge is out!"

"Okay," said the tricycle driver, "I cannot fix the bridge."

Page 8

A policeman warned the earth-mover driver, "Go back! The bridge is out!"

"No, I will not go back," said the earth-mover driver. "I *can* fix the bridge!"

Page 9

"Hooray!" shouted the tractor driver.
"Hooray!" shouted the fire truck driver.
"Hooray!" shouted the ice cream truck driver.
"Hooray!" shouted the cement truck driver.
"Hooray!" shouted the motorcycle driver.
"Hooray!" shouted the tricycle driver.

Page 10

"We cannot fix the bridge, but the earth-mover driver *can!*" Everyone shouted.

Page 11

The policeman waved his arm, "Go ahead, earth-mover driver! Fix the bridge!"

The policewoman waved her arm, "Go ahead, earth-mover driver! Fix the bridge!"

Page 12

The earth-mover driver waved to the policeman.
The earth-mover driver waved to the policewoman.

Page 13

He waved to the tractor driver.
He waved to the fire truck driver.
He waved to the ice cream truck driver.
He waved to the cement truck driver.
He waved to the motorcycle driver.
He waved to the tricycle driver.

Page 14

Then the earth-mover driver went to work.

Page 15

More earth-mover drivers and workers came to the bridge that was out.

The policeman waved his arm, "Go ahead! Go and fix the bridge!"

The policewoman waved her arm, "Go ahead! Go and fix the bridge!"

Page 16

The earth-mover drivers did go ahead.

They went to work to fix the bridge.

Page 17

Every day the policeman said to the drivers, "Go back! The bridge is out!"

Every day the policewoman said to the drivers, "Go back! The bridge is out!"

Page 18

Every day the earth-mover drivers worked.

Every day they moved earth to fix the bridge.

It took a long time.

Page 19

One day the policeman waved his arm at the tractor driver, "Go ahead! You can cross the bridge!"

The tractor driver said, "I can?"

Page 20

That day the policeman waved his arm at the fire truck driver, "Go ahead! You can cross the bridge!"

The fire truck driver said, "I can?"

Page 21
The policewoman waved her arm at the ice cream truck driver, "Go ahead! You can cross the bridge!"
The ice cream truck driver said, "I can?"

Page 22
The policewoman waved her arm at the cement truck driver, "Go ahead! You can cross the bridge!"
The cement truck driver said, "I can?"

Page 23
The policewoman waved her arm at the motorcycle driver, "Go ahead! You can cross the bridge!"
The motorcycle driver said, "I can?"

Page 24
The policeman waved his arm at the tricycle driver, "Go ahead! You can cross the bridge!"
The tricycle driver said, "I can?"

Page 25
"Oh, look!" shouted the tricycle driver. "Look at the bridge!"
Everyone looked at the bridge.
The bridge—

Page 26
was FIXED!
(The last picture shows all drivers on the span of the bridge.)

Appendix E

Sample of an Illustrated Patterned Book: What Do I Pet?

The following pages have illustrations and text that can be photocopied, colored, and pasted on the pages of a two-sheet Bindless Book (see appendix F).

The text is first grade level.

What Do I Pet?

This book was colored by:

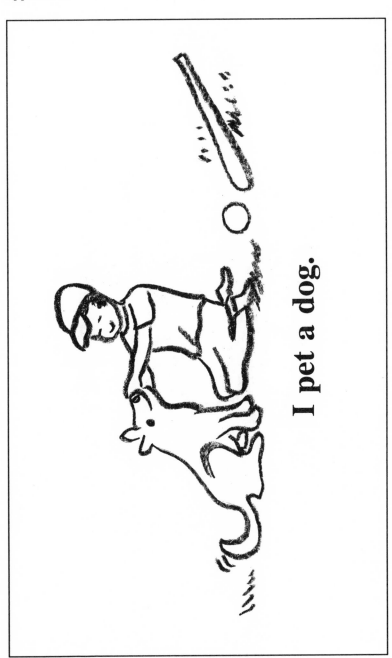

I pet a dog.

I pet a cat.

I pet a rabbit.

I pet a duck.

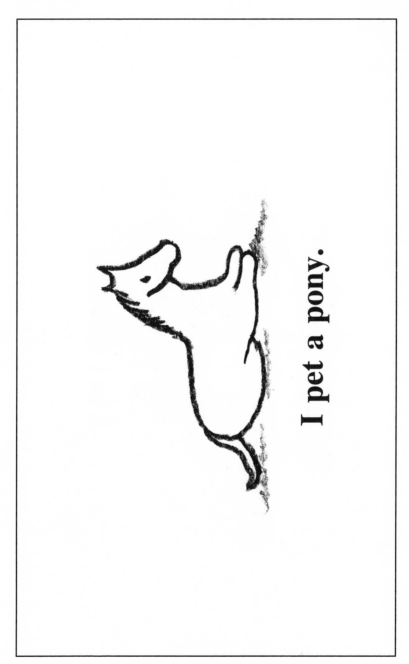

I pet a pony.

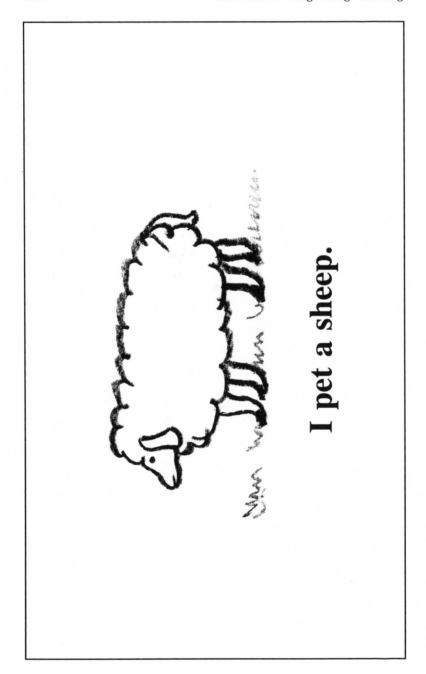

I pet a sheep.

Appendix F

How to Make a Bindless Book[1]

Bindless books require no staples, tape, glue, nor thread, and their page numbers can vary in length. Each sheet of paper provides two half sheets, front and back, or four book pages. If desired, finished books can be disassembled easily and laminated for longer wear.

1. Fold two 8 1/2" x 11" sheets of paper in half with short edges touching.

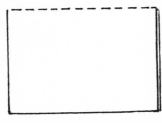

---

[1]The Bindless Book is similar to the "slit book" in *Read! Write! Publish!* published by Creative Teaching Press.

2. Cut a narrow slit along the fold line of one of the folded sheets of paper, beginning 1" from one edge and ending 1" from the opposite edge. The paper will still be in one piece.

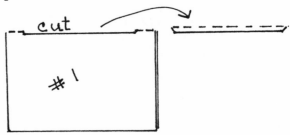

3. Cut rounded corners on the short sides of the second folded sheet, beginning 1" from the long side opposite the fold line.

4. Unfold the second sheet; roll it lengthwise, and slide it halfway through the long slit in the first sheet.

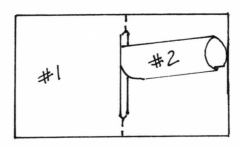

5. Reopen the second sheet so that its rounded corners ease into the slit in the first sheet, holding both sheets in place.

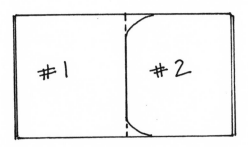

Glossary

Automaticity is an appropriate pace of reading which is instant, fluent, and free-flowing.

Basal method uses basal readers from grades one through eight. Teachers who use this method have traditionally followed the teacher's guide, which often suggests teaching one or two stories per week. If a student reads ahead, some teachers chide, "Don't peek ahead! Nobody goes ahead without my direction." These teachers worry that they must make the book last all year. They also tend to be upset when they receive a student who has already read the reader for the grade level they currently teach. Many teachers "get around" this problem by allowing bright students to read ahead in a different basal series from the one being used by their district.

Basal readers are books that are part of a graded set that has carefully sequenced, incremental vocabulary development. Publishers sell their series (such as the old Scott Foresman *Dick and Jane* series), along with teachers' guides and supplemental helps, to schools. Although many schools are now departing from this tradition, many children still read the same story in the same book throughout the school year. Some teachers, feeling the stilted vocabulary in basals renders them dull, opt for the richer, more descriptive (and often more difficult) passages found in children's literature.

Comprehension means understanding what one reads. Some students can pronounce and decode words they have heard but do not understand; i.e., they do not comprehend what they read.

Decoding includes whatever strategies a reader uses to unscramble a word, such as the following:

1. *Does it look right?* (identifies the sound the letter starts with. More mature readers also check vowel and ending sounds).

2. *Does it make sense?* (ascertains whether the word has meaning in its context).

3. *Does it sound right?* (checks whether the word is correct English usage—would we say it that way?)

Emergent literacy is a state of readiness to read and also a method to promote reading awareness via participation in prereading activities such as acquiring vocabulary; viewing print on billboards, TV, road signs, and cereal boxes; being read to; coloring in books; and watching others read.

Emergent reading is a stage in which students begin noticing print; i.e., they recognize letters, numbers, shapes of words, and/or words in places such as store and street signs, food labels, and favorite books.

Fluency is reading at a rate at which the student comprehends easily.

Frustration level is a very tough, highly specialized, and too difficult level of reading, such as when a fourth grader wishes to read a manual for fixing a car or when an illiterate person wants to read income tax forms. At frustration level, readers often cannot pronounce or decode the vocabulary. If they can read the words, they may not comprehend their meaning.

Independent reading level is the level of reading at which readers understand and recognize approximately 98% of the vocabulary and need little or no help, such as when a reader rereads a story he or she has already learned or when fifth grade students choose library books that they can read fluently when checked by the Middle-of-the-Book Test (see chapter 3). Students reading at their independent level occasionally find a word they do not know, but this occasional word usually does not inhibit overall comprehension.

Instructional level is a level of reading at which a reader needs some support or prereading help with new words, such as the next story that follows the one just learned in the basal reader or a selection in which a student can read most of the words but needs help with some words in order to comprehend the story. Readers at the instructional level may read haltingly and with partial comprehension on the first reading, but fluency, word recognition, and comprehension increase on the second and third readings.

Literature is a term used loosely by many teachers to mean anything from books that are not basals to those that have won awards. Many teachers use high quality children's literature that has been adapted to lower reading levels in graded reading textbooks. Others supplement with library or other books chosen to reflect a theme.

Literature-based instruction can exclude all resources from the reading program save good books and environmental reading (purist approach, often individualized) or may include modifications such as teacher reading literature to the whole class, reading skills instruction, supplementary basal reading, and/or thematic instruction.

Phonics is a method of learning the sounds of letters and unscrambling a word by examining its letter sounds: beginning, middle, and end.

Reading is a process of simultaneously seeing, hearing, and understanding a word automatically.

Rereading is practicing reading the same passages repeatedly, using a variety of techniques, until achieving automaticity.

Sighting a word is encountering it. The word needs to be read over and over within a short enough time frame so that the word is not forgotten between sightings.

Thematic instruction is teaching any or all subjects in the context of a theme; i.e., if the theme is "water," instruction might include experimentation with floating objects, ice, and steam, and reading about water or water animals. Studying words in meaningful contexts enhances comprehension and interest.

Whole language sometimes means integration of reading with other language arts (spelling, writing, grammar). The term "whole language" can also mean teaching skills in the context of a whole passage (i.e., teaching the sound of the letter "m" in a shared reading experience with a big book). Often whole language methods are integrated with other subjects within a theme.

References

Adams, M. J. 1994. *Beginning to read: Thinking and learning about print.* Cambridge, MA: The MIT Press.

Dublin, P., H. Pressman, and E. J. Woldman. 1994. *Integrating computers in your classroom: Elementary language arts.* New York: HarperCollins.

Fielding, L., and C. Roller. 1992. Making difficult books accessible and easy books acceptable. *The Reading Teacher 45:* 678–85.

Fry, E. 1994. *1000 Instant Words: The most comon words for teaching reading, writing, and spelling.* Laguna Beach, CA: Laguna Beach Educational Books.

Geough, P. B. 1972. One second of reading. In *Language by ear and by eye,* edited by J. F. Kavanagh and I. G. Mattingly. Cambridge, MA: The MIT Press.

Gunning, T. G. 1994. *Creating reading instruction for all children.* Boston: Allyn and Bacon.

Hammond, W. D. 1983. How your students can predict their way to reading comprehension. *Learning 12*(4): 63–4.

Kessler, L. 1961. *The duck on the truck.* New York: Wonder Books.

Martin, J. G. 1968. Temporal word spacing and the perception of ordinary, anomalous, and scrambled strings. *Journal of Verbal Learning and Verbal Behavior 7:* 1954–57.

Myers, M. L. and C. J. Oliphant. 1994. Sustained silent reading: A fresh approach. *Wisconsin State Reading Association Journal 38*(3): 39–43.

Peterson, B. n.d. Selecting books for beginning readers. Unpublished ms. Columbus: Ohio State University.

Topping, K. 1989. Peer tutoring and paired reading: combining two powerful techniques. *The Reading Teacher 42:* 488.

————. 1987. Paired reading: A powerful technique for parent use. *The Reading Teacher 40:* 604–14.

Wilson, P. T. 1988. *Let's think about reading and reading instruction: A primer for tutors and teachers.* Dubuque, IA: Kendall Hunt.

Bibliography

Aukerman, R. 1984. *Approaches to beginning reading.* New York: Wiley.

Aycock, H. 1990. Compute! Choice: Develop problem-solving skills and have fun, too. *Compute 12*(3): 68–71.

Bitter, G. 1983. Computer software roundup. *Instructor and Teacher 93*(4): 94–99.

Blanchard, J. S., G. E. Mason, and D. Daniel. 1987. *Computer applications in reading.* 3rd ed. Newark, DE: International Reading Association.

Brawer, J. 1989. Reading Magic Library. *A+ 7*(2): 93–95.

Clay, M. M. 1991. *Becoming literate: The construction of inner control.* Portsmouth, NH: Heinemann.

————. 1985. *The early detection of reading difficulties.* Auckland, New Zealand: Heinemann.

Coody, B. 1992. *Using literature with young children.* Dubuque, IA: Wm. C. Brown Publishers.

Cullen, S. 1988. Product roundup. *A+ 6*(4): 118–123.

Dardig, J. 1988. At-home activities for beginning readers. *Instructor 98*(4): 84.

Diaz-Lefevre, R. 1990. "I just didn't have enough time...": Assisting the busy adult learner develop critical reading and thinking skills. *Adult Learning 2*(1): 30–32.

Durkin, D. 1993. *Teaching them to read.* 6th ed. Boston: Allyn and Bacon.

Eiser, L. 1993. Bailey's Book House. *Technology & Learning 14*(1): 8–10.

————. 1991. Discis Books. *Technology & Learning 11*(8): 8–10.

Fry, E. 1992. *How to teach reading: For teachers, parents, tutors.* Laguna Beach, CA: Laguna Beach Educational Books.

Gipe, J., and J. C. Richards. 1992. Activating background knowledge: Strategies for beginning and poor readers. *The Reading Teacher 45:* 474–478.

Gitelman, H. F. 1990. Using wordless picture books with disabled readers. *The Reading Teacher 43:* 525.

Glazer, S. M., and E. M. Burke. 1994. *An integrated approach to early literacy.* Boston: Allyn and Bacon.

Goldenberg, C. 1991. Learning to read in New Zealand: The balance of skills and meaning. *Language Arts 68:* 555–563.

Goodman, Y. M., ed. 1990. *How children construct literacy: Piagetian perspectives.* Newark, DE: International Reading Association.

Gould, T. 1991. *Get ready to read: A practical guide for teaching young children at home and in school.* New York: Walker.

Hall, S. 1990. *Using picture storybooks to teach literary devices: Recommended books for children and young adults.* Phoenix, AZ: Oryx Press.

Hart-Hewins, L., and J. Wells. 1990. *Real books for reading: Learning to read with children's literature.* Portsmouth, NH: Heinemann.

International Reading Association. 1986. *How to prepare materials for new literates.* Newark, DE: International Reading Association.

Iversen, S., and W. Tunmer. 1993. Phonological processing skills and the reading recovery program. *Journal of Educational Psychology 85*(1): 112.

Keefe, D., and D. Meyer. 1988. Profiles of instructional strategies for adult disabled readers. *Journal of Reading 31:* 614–620.

Laughlin, M., and C. L. Swisher. 1990. *Literature-based reading: Children's books and activities to enrich the K–5 curriculum.* Phoenix, AZ: Oryx Press.

LeVitus, B. 1993. Easy reader. *MacUser 9*(5): 215–219.

Martin, J. 1982. Cloze reading skills. *Instructor and Teacher 91* (8): 113.

Mason, J., and J. Allen. 1986. *A review of emergent literacy with implications for research and practice in reading.* Champaign, IL: University of Illinois at Urbana-Champaign.

Morrow, L. M. 1993. *Literacy development in the early years: Helping children read and write.* Boston: Allyn and Bacon.

Norton, D. 1992. *The impact of literature-based reading.* New York: Merrill.

Olenoski, S. 1992. Using jump rope rhymes to teach beginning reading skills. *The Reading Teacher 46:* 173–176.

Palmer, W. 1987. Try rehearsed reading. *Instructor 97*(1): 75.

Parham, C. 1992. Stories and more. *Technology & Learning 12*(4): 17–19.

———. 1991. S-P-E-L-L: The reading/writing connection. *Technology & Learning 11*(6): 8–10.

Rauch, S. J., and J. Sanacore, eds. 1985. *Handbook for the volunteer tutor.* 2d ed. Newark, DE: International Reading Association.

Reutzel, D. R., and R. Cooter. 1992. *Teaching children to read: From basals to books.* New York: Merrill.

Rieben, L., and C. A. Perfetti, eds. 1991. *Learning to read: Basic research and its implications.* Hillsdale, NJ: L. Erlbaum Associates.

Rosen, M. 1991. A parent's best gift. *Reader's Digest 139*(831): 29–33.

Rosenberg, L., M. Kohn, V. Monroe, and J. Spencer. 1993. Best new books, music and videos for life. *Parents' Magazine 68*(3): 69–73.

Samuels, S. J., ed. 1978. *What research has to say about reading instruction.* Newark, DE: International Reading Association.

Saul, W., and S. A. Jagusch, eds. 1992. *Vital connections: Children, science, and books.* Papers from a symposium sponsored by the Children's Literature Center. Portsmouth, NH: Heinemann.

Stanton, D. 1989. Give your child's reading skills a big boost—turn on the computer. *Compute! 11*(3): 15.

Stephens, E., ed. 1990. *What matters?: A primer for teaching reading.* Portsmouth, NH: Heinemann.

Stoll, D. R., ed. 1990. *Magazines for children.* Glassboro, NJ: International Reading Association.

Strickland, D. S., and L. M. Morrow. 1989. Developing skills: An emergent literacy perspective. *The Reading Teacher 43:* 82–84.

————, eds. 1989. *Emerging literacy: Young children learn to read and write.* Newark, DE: International Reading Association.

Trachtenburg, P., and A. Ferruggia. 1989. Big books from little voices: Reaching high risk beginning readers. *The Reading Teacher 42:* 284–290.

Unzicker, C. E. 1934. *An experimental study of the effect of the use of the typewriter on beginning reading.* New York: Teachers College, Columbia University.

Venditto, G. 1988. Stepping stones: Learning from pictures. *PC Magazine 7*(3): 442.

Vilscek, E. C., ed. 1968. *A decade of innovations: Approaches to beginning reading.* Newark, DE: International Reading Association.

Williams, R. T., ed. 1976. *Insights into why and how to read.* Newark, DE: International Reading Association.

Index

About the Author

Marie L. Myers, Ph.D., an experienced professor of teacher education, specializes in innovative teaching methods. She is currently adapting beginning reading and mathematics methodologies to bilingual education.